WHAT DOES IT TAKE?

PASTOR JACK MCKEE

BELFAST

WHAT DOES IT TAKE?

Published by Maurice Wylie Media, Bethel Media House, Tobermore, Magherafelt, Northern Ireland BT45 5SG (UK)

Publishers' statement: Throughout this book the love for our God is such that whenever we refer to Him we acknowledge with Capitals. On the other hand when referring to the devil we refuse to acknowledge him with any honour to the point of violating the grammatical rule of a withheld capital.

www.mauricewyliemedia.com

Create | Brand | Establish

Contents

ENDORSEMENTS

Many people have heard of or seen the struggles and conflicts in Northern Ireland and wondered what could be done. One man, called of Jesus accepted the challenge and the call. With total focus on Jesus, the Cross and people he has and is making a great impact in Belfast and on to the world. This book *'What Does It Take?'* will rock your world. Warning 'you too may become a radical follower of Jesus'. Great book my friend Jack, so proud of you and you lifting up the cross and Jesus!

A servant, pilgrim follower of Jesus and fellow cross carrier,

Arthur Blessitt,

'Pray and don't give up' (Luke 18:1).

When you have stood and faced death, had people shoot at you, and had your car bombed and destroyed, and you stand with a cross while people mock you, and your church is right smack dab in the middle of a major conflict zone, and you still go on, I believe you have the authority by God to write a book called 'What Does it Take?'

I have known Jack McKee for many years now and when I came to minister at his church, New Life City Church, there is one word that could best describe the author of this book and the Pastor of that church, Pioneer.

If you want to know how to lay a hold of Jesus and continue to run the race in the face of opposition, this book is a MUST READ. I know that it will inspire you and build your faith to stand for Jesus Christ in your generation now.

Roy Fields USA, Evangelist & Worship Leader

Having known Pastor Jack McKee for over 25 years I count it a privilege to write these few words regarding his latest book.

'What Does It Take?' Is a compelling read; a gripping account of his journey over 33 years of ministry in the complex and troubled city of Belfast. Beyond the pages you will pick up the heartbeat of a man of God who has been deeply impacted by the truth that the real church exists not only to worship but also to be a voice and an irrepressible influence for change in a seriously messed up world.

Jack's unique story is a reminder that living in pursuit of a God-given dream does not mean exemption from personal danger, disappointment or hard work. His hands-on approach to evangelism has taken him and the church he leads right onto the peace line between two deeply divided communities in Belfast, where he continues to witness first-hand the amazing transformational power that is released through the message of the cross.

As you read, prepare to be challenged, and I pray you will be inspired by the pioneering spirit that leaps from these pages.

Pastor Edwin Michael Superintendent of the Elim Church in Ireland

Pastor Jack McKee has worked for a lifetime in North and West Belfast. Having first-hand knowledge, I consider this a compelling story of courage, about someone who has served not in an area ripe for success, but on the edge, in a community of mixed loyalties, torn asunder by over thirty years of violence.

Working on the Belfast peace line is not a comfortable place to be. Here, Jack has stood the test of opposition. He will rightly acknowledge the support of the team of workers and the congregation of New Life City Church. However above all, it is the strengthening and anointing of the Holy Spirit that has enabled him to lift high the empty cross of the Lord Jesus Christ.

Rev. Jim Rea MBE Former President of the Methodist Church in Ireland

From the pages of this book two things are obvious, Pastor Jack's passion for his community and the focus with which he fulfills his service to the people. He pushes the mark, tests the boundaries and fearlessly (at least outwardly) confronts in the name of Jesus. The people of New Life City Church and of the Shankill region will know in eternity the difference this ministry has made in many lives. Thank you for serving our city.

Pastor Glenn Dunlop, Karmel City Church,
Belfast and former player for Crusaders Football Club, Northern Ireland.

When in Belfast, fresh from Bible College in New Zealand, God placed Jack McKee in my life and he changed it forever. Although I now pastor a church on the other side of the world, I am still proud to call this humble man my Pastor. He is the real deal, a role model for all of us, touching lives not only in his own community, but around the world. Unafraid to share the Gospel in the face of danger and adversity. We can all learn something from him.

Pastor Colin Morrison MMin, BMin, Dip B.S.

Senior Pastor – Elim Community Church, Invercargill, New Zealand

DEDICATION

I fully understand that I would not be where I am today without the love, support and the gifting of so many people. A goal is not scored by one person, but by a team united and committed to the same objective. I truly thank God for those who have stood with me, sometimes sacrificially, whether family, friends, volunteers, church members or leaders.

A special mention to my partner in life and ministry

I cannot possibly begin this book without first of all mentioning a very special person who has partnered with me through life, ministry, hard times and good times, and who has, without doubt, what it takes.

Kathleen started out in life as Catherine McDermott. Brought up in the narrow streets in a little place called Brown Square at the bottom end of the Shankill Road, she had no idea where life would lead when she was swept off her teenage feet by this good looking, red haired, young man she called Jackie.

We married on November 4, 1972. Less than four years later we had our first child Jonathan followed three years later by our daughter Chara (Cara) and another three years later by our second daughter Paula.

Kathleen has stood against so many things that words do not speak highly enough of who she is and what she is to me and to others. Often going beyond the normal expectations of a 'pastor's wife', by running a successful pre-school playgroup, besides an after-school club for children with additional needs; she bravely faced the death of one of these children who perished in a fire along with his father and grandmother. Reaching out to families evicted from their homes during serious community violence, while still finding time to reach out to children in Albania by organising and travelling with two 40ft containers filled with supplies.

I have seen her lift our children out of their beds and place them on blankets on our bedroom floor, so that young men in danger of being beaten or shot would have somewhere safe to stay. I have also seen her spending days cleaning up when our home was attacked by paramilitaries who smashed every window, and I've seen her live through the horror watching helplessly as her car burned to a shell after it had been fire-bombed during that same attack.

The fact remains that many young men are alive today because she opened her home as a safe place, and that many young men and young women, who started their early education at *Hobby Horse Playgroup*, that she personally pioneered, are now raising their own children within the wider community, with many returning with their children to the same playgroup they had attended when they too were toddlers. Many others across the community and beyond have received help way beyond the expected duty of a pastor's wife, and all because Kathleen McKee had, and still has, what it takes.

I am honoured to dedicate this book to Kathleen and to all those who have stood alongside us on our journey.

Jack

FOREWORD

It's not what I would have personally intended, yet I know I have become somewhat of an enigma to many of my contemporaries, both inside and outside the church. This has happened as I have sought to serve and reach my home community and those beyond, armed with nothing more than the Gospel of Jesus Christ, but in ways that many would deem unconventional.

I served as a soldier within the Ulster Defence Regiment (UDR) from 1972 until 1977. These were some of the darkest years in Northern Ireland's Troubles where murder claimed the lives of many through the gun and the bomb. Avoiding death several times while some of my close friends and colleagues were tragically murdered by terrorists, I chose to lay aside my military career for the greater cause of taking up the message of the cross, even to the point where I would end-up by literally taking up the cross and carrying it through some of Belfast's most notorious troubled streets.

In 1982 I began ministering in the heart of Troubles-ridden Belfast, reaching across the long-standing sectarian divide of Northern Ireland's conflict, touching both Protestant and Catholic alike. There, for over 40 years a 20 foot high concrete wall has stood Berlin-style between warring communities that have suffered much at each other's hands during years of civil conflict and terrorist activity. These communities have suffered the commonality of social deprivation and have painfully discovered the democracy of death that comes to all of us, regardless of age or of religious or political persuasion, yet they have all too often been hurt by those who live among us, who are bone of our bone and flesh of our flesh.

One of the most significant years in my entire ministry was 1989. This was a year that presented a major turning point for me as the pastor of a local church, even more so, as to how I would connect with the wider community in Belfast and beyond. It was during this year that enough funds were raised to purchase an old cinema, something I had never previously even considered, but it soon became obvious that it was part of God's plan to widen the ministry of the church. Now, rather than wait for the people to attend our Sunday services, we felt we could take the church to the people every day of the week. Soon, what had previously been a cinema was converted into a youth and community outreach centre, operated by a small team of employees and volunteers who facilitated programmes, projects and activities for all ages.

The main focus, however, was specifically directed at reaching young men and young women who were being affected not only by the normal inner city problems of drugs and alcohol, but also by the ongoing sectarian and internal community violence. Many young men being recruited into paramilitary organisations were as young as thirteen, and often fell victim to paramilitary godfathers resulting in punishment beatings and shootings, often leading to permanent injury and sometimes death.

Another significant year was 1993, with the launch of New Life City Church as a direct response to the spiritual needs of young people who were finding safety within our new outreach centre. However, due to issues and difficulties with the structural condition of the building, the church and community outreach programmes had to move out in 1999. Due to local political and paramilitary influences, we were unable to move back. After several moves we were finally able to settle into our new home in 2009, a large warehouse that we had managed to purchase in 2006. Our new premises is a building that literally straddles the main dividing line between the conflicting communities in Belfast, with half of the building on one side of the divide and half on the other side, giving us the unique privilege, as a church, of having a cornerstone on each side of the divide. This surely was God at work!

However, while God had clearly set this up, the devil was at work in the background to dishearten and attempt to prevent the advancement of our ministry. We faced criticism from other churches and from other Christians who failed to understand our heart and our sense of God's call in relation to our outreach work in the wider community. We also attracted negative responses from local terrorist organisations who failed to show appreciation for any public condemnation of their violent activities. Some of these responses will be explained later in this book.

Each year I would spend up to three months ministering in the USA, speaking in schools and churches and other venues. I have often been asked why I stay in Northern Ireland and have been encouraged to move somewhere safer like the Bronx in New York! My reply has always been the same: "There is no better place to be, no more exciting place to be, and no safer place to be, than right where God has placed you, right in the centre of God's will."

That better place, that exciting place, that safer place, is not necessarily the church building or the church platform, but could also be the streets and in the heart of conflict and danger, if that's where God has you.

This book will take you from the indoor safety zone of what many perceive to be normal church life, to the spiritual battlefields that exist just outside the front door of every church.

INTRODUCTION

When someone I have known personally, worked with, or have led to faith in Christ, is victimised, beaten or murdered due to the ongoing paramilitary and terrorist violence here in Northern Ireland. Am I going to simply climb the steps to the safety of the church platform and preach my next sermon, or am I going to step up and step outside the feel good 'safe' place? It is there, I'll see that God is not only bigger than the traditions of the church, but He's much bigger than our fears and those who would seek to intimidate and threaten, and cut asunder the religious red-tape that has been placed around us.

Several years ago, as a pastor, I made the conscious decision to live my life worthy of His calling. I knew that each day might bring new challenges and even troubles, but I knew that what the Lord started in me in 1967, He would not have ignited, if He could not have followed through with it. And it's the same with you!

"Being confident of this, that he who began a good work in you will carry it on to completion until the day of Christ Jesus." Philippians 1:6.

I concluded several years ago that it's not more songs or sermons we need, but it's more of God. The reason you are reading this book is that you sense the same thing in your heart. Have you got what it takes to be the Church that Christ intended it to be?

Pastor Jack McKee

Chapter 1

A Defining Decade

Although a child of the *Fabulous Fifties*, I am more a product of the *Swinging Sixties*. It was not only the decade in which I became a teenager, but was the decade which set my taste for music and confirmed my passion for one of the greatest football teams in European history - Liverpool Football Club. It was also the decade that I smoked my first cigarette, had my first taste of alcohol, committed my first break-in at one of the local pubs, went on my first shoplifting expedition, gambled on my first card game, placed my first bet on a racehorse, finished with school, took on my first full-time job, and dated my first serious girlfriend, Kathleen McDermott, to whom I have been happily married since 1972. It was also the decade in which I committed my life to following Jesus Christ.

Prior to the 1960s, Belfast was virtually unknown outside the island of Ireland. Although the city and the country made a huge contribution to achieving victory in Europe during World Wars I and II, and although it received its share of deadly metallic packages delivered by Hitler's Luftwaffe, killing hundreds of its inner city residents, yet its most noteworthy pre-1960s achievement was the building of the Titanic! However, before the end of the 1960s, Belfast would take its place on the world stage along with Berlin and Beirut, but sadly for the same tragic reasons.

The 1960s in Belfast were ushered in by the new sound of the *Swinging Sixties*, but ended with the slaughter of many of its sons and daughters in bloody acts of violence. This was not violence inflicted by the Luftwaffe or by any other outside force, but by elements within the city itself, as neighbour turned against neighbour and community against community. The hostility was not confined to Belfast alone, but quickly spread across Northern Ireland.

Having committed my life to Christ in 1967, my first few years as a new Christian had gone almost unchallenged, except for the odd catcall and name-calling by several of my then social friends. However, the real challenge to my faith came with the outbreak of Northern Ireland's conflict that affected every street in our community. Like many, on both sides of the conflict, I felt overwhelmed by a sense of fear, but also by a compelling force to get involved. As a 17-year-old, I had little understanding of what was going on. All I knew at that time was that Protestants and Catholics were fighting against each other and that I had been raised a Protestant.

The extent and the severity of the initial outbreak of violence took most by surprise. It brought an immediate response of participation from those on both sides of the conflict who believed they had to take a stand for their respective side. Even as a committed Christian, and a young, impressionable one at that, I also felt it was my duty to get involved by going onto the streets and participating in the conflict. What began as an outbreak of violence that year developed into a long-term conflict that became known as 'The Troubles'.

It wasn't long before the government issued instructions for a 20ft high concrete wall to be built between the communities in an attempt to keep them apart. The purpose of this wall was to make it difficult for opposing factions to attack each other, but it did not stop the murder squads who committed random attacks against the 'other' community, sometimes taking out specific targets, or by planting bombs in public places across the city, leaving a trail of death, brokenness, mistrust and destruction.

As the Troubles embedded themselves, those living on both sides of the dividing wall retreated to the safety of their respective communities. Life became much more entrenched as many chose to live, work and socialise as much as possible, within their own neighbourhood. This not only created an opportunity for the emergence of paramilitary/terrorist organisations, but also resulted in generations where many were not only fearful of those on 'the other side', but had little or no contact at all with them.

The *Swinging Sixties* might well have begun with the sound of rock and roll heard on every transistor radio, but for the people of Belfast, and of Northern Ireland, the Sixties were going out to the sound of the bomb and the bullet, that would soon leave many as real victims of the conflict. The violence was also about to knock on my door!

Chapter 2

Onward Christian Soldier

While many of my friends and family members were signing up to join the emerging paramilitary organisations, I knew that as a committed Christian I could never consider joining any of these groups, yet I felt I needed to do something. So in 1972 I joined the Ulster Defence Regiment (UDR), which today is called the Royal Irish Regiment (RIR). The UDR was a regiment within the British Army and was made up of recruits from Northern Ireland, with up to 10,000 at any one time, full-time and part-time. I signed up for five years of active military service.

While on patrol with the UDR it was our role to provide support and backup for the police and the British Army who were often stretched and under pressure from the ever-increasing murderous terrorist campaign. Besides defending utility installations being targeted by terrorists, we were active on the ground in setting up roadblocks, stopping and searching vehicles, and assisting with evacuations during bomb alerts. However, as the UDR consisted mainly of people who lived at home and travelled to our base camps by car or on foot, it made us vulnerable and easy targets for terrorist organisations from both communities, but especially to those who were anti-British, as we were a regiment within the British Army.

As a Christian I always sought God for direction and prayed

Onward Christian Soldier   19

for protection for myself, my friends and my family, but I always knew that I still needed to be cautious. The fact was, people were being killed, and that included Christians. I knew I needed to pray, but I also knew I needed to be wise and prepared for any eventuality. I had no idea just how soon after joining the UDR I would be looking to God for protection, whilst at the same time using what little wisdom and common sense I had.

On a dark and cold October evening in 1972, just a few weeks before my wedding, I found I needed God's protection. That night, although I was the proud owner of a motorbike, I was making my way home on foot along an interface area close to my home in Denmark Street. I had just parted from friends in the Oldpark area of Belfast when suddenly – a gunman was in front of me. I could not see his face. I had no idea who he was, or what age he could be. All I knew was - he blocked my path and had a weapon in his hand.

That moment when he raised the gun and pointed it directly at me, time seemed to slow right down. I had often played out in my mind how I might react if ever I was faced with such a situation. In my mind's eye I would quickly draw a weapon and open fire, thereby killing the would-be assassin and saving myself, but in reality, that only works if you are armed. On this particular night, I was not carrying a legally issued firearm, so I did the next best thing – I ran! As I did so, five shots rang out, but I knew that for as long as I could still hear the shots, I was okay, I was still alive!

I instinctively ran towards a street that I knew was Protestant. I knew I would be safe there. That was my side of the divide. While running frantically for my life, I could see a hand stretched around a corner and on seeing a black glove and black sleeve I knew it was the hand of a police constable. I grabbed hold of that hand and moments later, I was pulled to safety.

The years I served in the UDR were difficult years, yet they were some of the most precious years of my life. The friendships and camaraderie were of the highest quality, especially given the fact that we depended upon each other in 'life and death' situations. There were also those times when we experienced great job satisfaction when successful in our fight against terrorism and especially in the saving of lives.

On a busy shopping afternoon, while I was driving the lead military Land Rover through Glengormley, a suburb on the outskirts of North Belfast, I noticed an unmanned car suspiciously parked at the front of a row of shops. My concern was raised by the fact that the car was obviously carrying extra weight. Its back-end was almost touching the ground, which is a tell-tale sign of a possible homemade car bomb - a favourite weapon of terrorists, often used to devastating effect.

As soon as I raised concern to our patrol commander who was beside me, he immediately agreed to check it out. Within moments we were in shops asking if anyone owned the car. Someone said they had seen a man park the car and get into another car and drive off. Upon hearing this we immediately evacuated the area. Our patrol blocked off the road at both ends and we then contacted the police and our headquarters to inform them of the situation and to call for military backup. Within twenty minutes the military bomb disposal team, nicknamed 'Felix' (the cat with nine lives), was with us. After assessing the situation, the bomb disposal officer, clad in heavy body armour and with his face covered by a heavy visor, slowly approached the car.

Still not knowing if there was a bomb, we watched from a short distance, but were concerned for the life of the officer approaching the car. As he neared the suspect vehicle, it suddenly exploded. The officer was blown right off his feet. We instinctively lunged underneath our Land Rover as debris and glass rained down upon us. It was over in seconds. Soon we were back on our feet, relieved to see that no one had been injured, and especially happy that no lives had been lost that day. Even Felix was back on his feet wiping the sweat from off his brow, and very much aware that on this occasion he had lost one of his nine lives.

Chapter 3

The Shadow of Death Comes Close

During those years I had read several books written by David Wilkerson, founder of Teen Challenge, a drug rehabilitation outreach with more than 200 centres across the USA and around the world. His books and work had made a deep impression on my life and had helped bring me to the place where I finally made the decision to leave the UDR and attend Bible College. Something inside of me wanted to be like David Wilkerson. In fact, I wanted to be to Belfast, what David Wilkerson had been to Brooklyn, New York. He had become my example, the one I wanted to emulate. So in February 1977, I applied to the Elim Bible College in England, and was accepted to attend in September of that year.

A few months before leaving for college, my friend and I were told that our names were on the 'hit list' of a terrorist organisation, the Irish Republican Army (IRA); a list was discovered by police in a home in North Belfast. At first I was shocked, wondering how they could have even known who I was. I then began to recall colleagues and friends who had been murdered by this same organisation, especially by IRA units based in North Belfast, where one my friends, Robert (Bobby) McComb, had been taken and tortured and finally shot through the head. So yes I, and my friend whose name was Michael Riley, took this information very seriously. We were shocked and angry, but not fearful, although we knew we would need to make a few changes regarding our personal security.

Michael's home was directly opposite mine, so we were neighbours as well as friends. We would travel together in my car when we were going to and from our base camp in North Belfast where we served together in the UDR. Our long-term service in the regiment was the reason our names appeared on this list. However, in spite of the fact that we had been named as potential IRA targets, we were simply told by the police to be careful. Michael and I began to take extra security precautions, and were coping well, yet the attack still happened.

Michael and I would normally meet at 3.30am outside his front door, then we walked to my car that was parked at the end of our street. One morning, thirty minutes before we were due to meet, I was disturbed by a noise in the street. I looked out from my bedroom window and I noticed Michael looking out at the same time. As we peered along the darkened street we could see someone standing right next to my car and a second person on his back, his body protruding out from underneath the vehicle. I was certain I had not ordered an early morning exhaust fit or an oil change, so Michael and I emerged from our homes with our guns drawn and on alert. We cautiously walked towards the car.

However, we were obviously not that light-footed, and on hearing and seeing us, the two guys bolted. With guns pointing in their direction, we challenged them to stop, but they kept on running. We did not fire after them, as we felt we were in no immediate danger, although some later suggested we should have opened fire, but that was not our style!

The two would-be assassins were in such a hurry they never even left a repair bill! However, they did leave an unsigned calling card in the form of tell-tale marks that enabled army personnel to confirm that an attempt had been made to attach a device underneath the car. This confirmed to both of us how seriously we should take the recent police warnings of the IRA threat to have us both killed.

Not long after this, in August 1977, Kathleen and I said farewell to the UDR and to Belfast, when we departed for Bible College in England. Towards the end of my first year at college, in June 1978, I received a phone call from my mother to tell me that Michael was critically injured after being shot by terrorists in his own home. He had been watching a football match on television when gunmen burst into his living room and shot him several times in the chest. Michael collapsed next to his baby daughter.

When my mother gave me the news, I hung up the phone and soon discovered that even at Bible College there was little comfort. We prayed for Michael and his family, with prayers that were mixed with tears. However, Michael died from his wounds two months later, in August 1978. This would not be the last time I would scream out and ask God: "How could you let this happen?"

Chapter 4

Into the Unknown

Having graduated from Bible College in June 1979, we immediately returned to Northern Ireland with Kathleen expecting our second child. Our first church appointment was to pastor a church in rural Rathfriland, with the additional responsibility of looking after a second church in Moneyslane. The churches were six miles apart and about 35 miles south of Belfast. At that time I had no idea where Rathfriland and Moneyslane were. I had to get a map of Northern Ireland to locate them.

We were delighted to be going back to Northern Ireland, but our hearts were very much in Belfast. We were city people, and no matter how much we tried we were never able to make the adjustment to rural life. We were there for two and a half years, during which time the Rathfriland church grew from around 50 regulars to around 90, while the Moneyslane church dropped from 18 to 17. We felt we had done quite well, but we wanted to return to Belfast, although we never thought we would be considered for a city church until we had been in the ministry for about 15 years. It seemed that city churches were in higher demand and were allocated to more experienced pastors and I was just a new kid on the block.

At the beginning of 1982 I was approached by the then superintendent of our denomination, Pastor Eric McComb, who told me of a church in Belfast that would soon become vacant and that our executive committee wanted me to meet with the leadership of that church with the view to moving from Rathfriland to Belfast. I remember being both shocked and excited by the prospect, and saying: "Eric, I'll need time to pray about this."

He said: "Take the next two weeks to think and pray about it, Jackie, and get back to me." Without allowing time for another breath I immediately said: "Eric, I've thought about it and I've prayed about it; I'll take it." I did not need another two weeks to pray for something I had already been praying about for two years.

Soon after I was sitting with the leadership, the church session, of Ballysillan Elim Church in North Belfast. There was an immediate heart-connection as we discussed calling and vision. It was all set. We would soon be returning not only to the city of Belfast, but returning to our home community; back to our turf where we knew many and where we also were known by many. We had no idea how more recognisable we would become in the years to follow.

We said farewell to the farming community and gladly returned to Belfast, totally oblivious to the fact that we were not only going back to an uncertain future, but one fraught with danger.

The early years were a breeze. We loved the church, loved the people, and loved what we were doing. We settled in quickly, and it wasn't long before we were making a difference in people's lives and also within the church. During the first few years we saw the church grow to such an extent that we had to knock down walls to enable us to bring in more seats. We were happy there, and if God had left us alone we could have stayed there. But God had other plans for us.

We were well into our seventh year, during 1989, when Kathleen was reading the local newspaper. This was the year when our lives would change direction once again. Who would have thought that reading a newspaper could change the direction of your life and ministry? Kathleen called out and said: "Jackie, the Stadium's for sale." This was an old cinema on the Shankill Road in Belfast. Many people went to this cinema to watch the amazing John Wayne beat Geronimo one week and then single-handedly win World War II the following week, while somewhere in-between he managed to find time to beat the tar out of Victor McLaglen in one of the most memorable fights ever seen on film, in the amazing 'The Quiet Man'.

So Kathleen was shouting out: "The Stadium's for sale," and I was thinking: "So what?" As a boy I could not even afford to purchase a ticket for an afternoon matinee. I was more often standing outside the Stadium watching people going in and coming out, than actually going inside to watch a film. So the thought never crossed my mind that this lad, who could not afford to purchase a ticket to go inside to watch a film, would one day actually buy the cinema.

For several days, I could not get the thought out of my mind that the Stadium was for sale. I began to believe that God was actually saying something to me, and that He was in fact directing me to the point where I would make an offer to purchase this building. I began to make enquiries, and soon discovered that others were interested in purchasing the old cinema. I also discovered that others connected with the Ulster Defence Association (UDA) and the Ulster Volunteer Force (UVF), both terrorist organisations within the Protestant community, were trying to prevent me from buying it. I was becoming a thorn in their flesh.

A leading member of the UVF wrote an article in a local newspaper hitting out against the idea of me buying the Stadium; stating that our community did not need another church, which I of course agreed with, but I wasn't looking to start another church. Later, while doing my pastoral hospital visitation, I met with one of the commanders of the North Belfast UDA who told me of the group's interest in purchasing the Stadium, even to the point of telling me what the organisation was offering, which was just over twice my bid. He suggested, in a friendly manner, that I withdraw my offer.

I had not even purchased the building, yet I was already facing opposition, which was a sign of things to come. By June 1989, against all the odds, we became the proud owners of the old Stadium cinema, and in September of that year we opened it under the new name of Stadium Youth and Community Centre. We had a specific outreach to 'at risk youths' within North and West Belfast, and it all started with Kathleen calling out: "Jackie, the Stadium is for sale."

Making a choice

For the next three years we established several youth clubs and programmes, as well as a pre-school playgroup, Hobby Horse Playgroup. At the same time I continued to pastor the church in Ballysillan, and did so for the next three years. After completing ten full years in this, my second church, I realised the time had come to make a choice; a choice between continuing to pastor the church, (where the people were more concerned that I was giving more time reaching out to the community via the Stadium and less personal time to them), or leave the church and work full-time at managing and developing outreach.

While it felt as if I was about to step off a cliff edge, or that I was stepping out of the boat to walk on uncharted waters, I chose to leave the church to which I had devoted the past decade of my life. Like Peter, I was leaving the security of the boat behind, and like Abraham, I did not know where I was going. I knew I was heading just a few miles south of Ballysillan, but I did not know where such a small move would eventually lead.

I knew I was leaving the church I'd been pastoring for ten years, and that I had no intention of pastoring another church. However, I was not leaving the ministry, but instead taking a different direction. This was my must needs moment, just like it was said of Jesus, *"He must needs go through Samaria"* (John 4:4), I felt in my spirit that I needed to take this step, a feeling that was helped along by the following two reasons.

The first one being that my commitment as pastor of the church was being questioned, perhaps with some justification as I was focusing more on the one that was lost than on the 99 that were safe, but it was enough to put me in the position of having to make the choice between looking after the church or reaching out to the wider community.

The second reason was that for a number of years I had felt trapped by the pastoral ministry. It was not that I believed I was not good at what I was doing; in fact I felt the very opposite. My pastoral calling and gifting was not in question. I believed I could preach a good word and pray a good prayer. I could visit the sick in hospital and people in their homes where I'd drink coffee and eat cake. I could officiate at weddings, funerals and infant dedications. In fact, I was becoming quite the professional, yet for all that, I still felt trapped and felt that something was missing.

I knew there was much more to the ministry than standing behind a lectern and thumping out a message of love on the one hand, and damnation on the other. The Stadium gave me the opportunity to break free and become involved in the type of evangelism that touches people where they are. I do not say this as a criticism of fellow pastors, but I believe we must find our own unique DNA in Christ, which can be the opposite of the recognised norm.

The more I sought God regarding this new direction, the more He impressed upon my heart the fact that there was a world beyond the four walls of every church building; a world that was vastly untouched by church that generally seems to live and function only within walls. I was feeling more and more uncomfortable, and even feeling a sense of guilt for not doing *"the work of an evangelist"* (2 Timothy 4:5). Preaching the Gospel to a room filled with Christians was not evangelism! I searched the Scriptures for the verse that commands the world to attend church buildings to hear us preach our sermons, sing our songs and watch us perform, but no matter how hard I searched, I could not find such a verse, because it's not there!

However, there is a verse in Matthew 28:18 that commands the church to *"go into all the world and preach the Gospel."* I suddenly felt free when I realised the world is not commanded to attend church, whereas Christians are commanded to be the church in the world! This became such a fresh revelation that it ultimately helped me make the decision to leave the security I had enjoyed for ten years as pastor of a growing church, and to develop a ministry that would reach those who are un-churched and often bypassed by the church.

Chapter 5

The Pain of Leaving

During our final months at Ballysillan Elim we faced our greatest trial and tragedy, something that no Bible College could train a person for. It was February 1992, we had already informed the church leadership that we were leaving to develop a ministry we believed would touch the lives of young people, particularly those being recruited and victimised by local paramilitary and terrorist organisations. However, just a few weeks before we were to formally leave the church, I was returning home one night after ministry when I saw a police roadblock close to our church building.

This sight was not unusual in Northern Ireland, and so I thought nothing of it. I took a detour and when I arrived home, Kathleen came running towards the car. She was crying, and through her tears she managed to say: "Jackie, Andy Johnston has been shot. I think he's dead." I can almost hear those words today. I immediately climbed back into the car and drove off towards the church to find out what had happened. I discovered it was true. The Irish People's Liberation Organisation (IPLO), another anti-British terrorist organisation, similar to the IRA, had murdered Andrew.

About Andrew...

I first met Andrew in 1982 when he was only a seven-year-old and had bright red hair and a freckled face. I often tell how I met him when he was seven, led him to faith in Christ when he was eleven, baptised him in water when he was fourteen, and then buried him when he was seventeen. Andrew had been watching the news on television when he saw a report that terrorists from the UDA had gone into a bookmaker's in Belfast and indiscriminately opened fire, tragically killing five Catholics.

Although from a Protestant background himself, Andrew began to weep as he listened to the report. With tears in his eyes he turned to his mother and said: "Why do people do these things and claim to be Protestant?" Sadly, and as if to underline the irony of Northern Ireland's conflict, in an act of direct retaliation for the above murders, Andrew Johnston was himself murdered and became another innocent victim of Northern Ireland's mad and senseless conflict.

Andrew had been working on that fateful Monday night, standing in for someone else, and thereby forgoing his normal Monday night meeting with his friends at our youth fellowship in church. At the exact moment they were playing guitars and singing and worshipping God, just several yards away, two men were walking from their car and stepping into a video shop where Andrew was working. Andrew noticed that one of the men was carrying a gun and immediately pushed his female colleague to the floor, but before he could take cover himself, he was shot twice in the chest.

There were no soldiers or police officers in the video store that Monday night who might have been legitimate targets. There were no members of any other paramilitary organisation in the store that night. There was only Andrew Johnston, age seventeen, and a female assistant, neither of whom had ever posed a threat to anyone. They were selected for no other reason than the fact that they were easy targets.

That night, when it was confirmed that Andrew had been murdered I got into my car and drove around the streets aimlessly. I wanted to get away from everyone, even from the Christians. I could not listen to the various comments, even though they were so well-meaning, especially those who said: "Well, at least he's with Jesus." Although I knew this to be true, I just did not want to hear it. His death was a tragedy, a crime, and the fact is, it should never have happened, Christian or not. It all seemed so utterly meaningless, and nothing could convince me that any good would be gained by the death of Andrew Johnston. So I drove off into the night. Alone.

Farewell to a young saint

I had been Andrew's pastor for ten years. I had watched him grow and develop into a young man who was an example to young people in his community and to other young people within the church, and now I had to deal with having to bury him as another victim of Northern Ireland's conflict. This would be one of my last responsibilities as pastor of Ballysillan Elim. Such thoughts were impossible to comprehend, so for 15 minutes, while driving around, I had what I can only describe as a mental blowout.

The amazing thing that night, was the incredible strength displayed by Andrew's mother, Yvonne. He was her only child, but while she felt the awful pain of such loss, she also displayed strength of character that was nothing less than supernatural. I remember saying to her: "Yvonne, I'm the Pastor, and I'm supposed to be saying these things to you!" She was a tremendous witness to the reality of God's abiding presence and to His incredible forgiveness.

Andrew's death touched the lives of many and actually created a brief lull in the violence at that time. A sense of horror swept through the entire community that one so young and so innocent should be so savagely cut down by an assassin's bullet. However, Andrew does not stand alone in terms of innocents being slaughtered by bloodthirsty assassins. He is simply representative of many, both Catholic and Protestant, young and old, male and female, whose futures on this earth were denied them.

The fact that Andrew's death touched many was evident in the numerous cards sent to his parents by both Protestants and Catholics. It was further evidenced by the massive turnout at his funeral as thousands lined the road as far as the eye could see. Many positive things were said about him at the funeral service, which was relayed from the packed church to those outside. When the coffin was carried from the church, many wept openly. One lady police officer was overcome with emotion as one of her male colleagues, a Catholic police officer, broke rank by taking some steps forward towards the coffin and poignantly saluting.

Andrew's future had been denied him by the violence of blind sectarianism that for too long had marred the moral landscape and gentle beauty of Ireland. The blood of its sons and daughters murdered by those who claim to be its liberators stains this island. Supporters of these agents of death, whether in the USA, Europe, or wherever else, have convinced themselves that those who kill in Ireland do so for a justifiable cause, but how tragically wrong they are, and how guilty they are in participating in and funding the deaths of innocents like Andrew Johnston.

Shortly after Andrew's death, his fiancée Julie Carville, my daughter Chara and their friend Elizabeth, were making their way home through a local housing estate, not far from our home. They had just passed a group of young men when suddenly they heard a shot ring out. They immediately turned to look behind them and saw a young man fall to the ground. He had been shot in the head. They watched in horror as the young man fell to the ground. The three young women were horrified and ran home, crying and screaming.

How sad that the youth of our nation, who were not responsible for this conflict, should nonetheless become its victims. How tragic that there are those among us who seem to be quite content with this scenario, as they seek to justify it as 'an inevitable consequence of the Troubles'. The youth of our nation are crying out for a better future, but those involved in terrorism, including Mafia-type organised crime, drug dealing, racketeering, and sex trafficking, do not only victimise our youth by physical punishment and death for various reasons, but by recruiting them, indoctrinating them, and using them, even from the age of thirteen.

Several weeks after Andrew's funeral, we eventually left Ballysillan Elim. It was like stepping out of an aquarium where fish are kept comfortably, and launching ourselves out into the wider ocean of humanity. We had no plan or intention of setting up another church. The UVF spokesperson I mentioned earlier was correct when he said: "The Shankill does not need another church!"

Church for the people

Often I have stated there are times when someone starts a church through a sense of calling and vision, and because the community needs the church, but there are times when someone starts it because they need the church and the position and title - it's more about them, and for them, than it is for the community.

What I felt our community needed then, and what the world needs today, is not just another church, but the church to be the church. Yes of course, we should provide opportunities for believers to come together so they can learn and grow, but we should also be coming together as followers of Jesus Christ for the purpose of going together, recognising we were never called to simply have church for Christians, but to be the church among those who are not yet Christians.

My focus was to reach the unreached and connect with the un-churched. I reached out through indoor sporting activities, facilitating personal development programmes, building an indoor climbing wall and a high-rope assault course, taking young men, young women, and ex-prisoners on outings and residentials, teaching as we went along. Our outings were not the normal church excursions, although I'm not suggesting there's anything wrong with church outings, but ours included adventures such as backpacking, bivouacking (the making of our own tents out of anything we could find in the forest and sleeping in it overnight), river rafting, caving, abseiling, and parachute jumping. These were the real 'legal highs' which offered the opportunity of connection, trust and communication.

While many of those who took part were not particularly religious, when it came to jumping from a plane, you can be sure that many of them spoke with God before taking that leap into nothingness. In fact even some of the Christians among us improved their prayer life during some of those activities. Then at the end of an activity, or at the end of a challenging day, there was ample opportunity to share life and faith stories while sitting around a campfire in the middle of a field, with only the open sky and stars above, answering several searching questions. I could see Jesus doing that. I felt at peace and knew I was on the right track.

It is not just about looking for opportunities to preach or impose our beliefs on others, but it's about meeting people at the very point of their need; it's about meeting people where they are. If someone is hungry we should feed them, and if someone is thirsty we should give them something to drink (preferably water), which sounds very much like the things Jesus did and would still do today. Yet, this was not just about food and water. This was about real life issues, and God knows there are many of those in all of our communities.

We have also gone beyond the point of just working with people from only one section of our divided community, to bringing people together from either side of the dividing wall that literally keeps them apart and separate from each other. The uniqueness of our cross-community work is that it does not take place in a safe environment, e.g. in neutral territory, but right in the heart of our communities. We have been amazed to see people, young and older, who would normally be fighting each other, working together to promote cooperation and a better understanding.

One of our personal development programmes, lasting several weeks, is called Higher Force Challenge, which recognises that within every person, regardless of who they are, there is a desire to improve and a longing for success. The programme has achieved recognition at various levels. Here are a few:

* A senior police officer commented, at one of our public presentation events: "Normally when my officers are involved with these young men, it's when they are arresting them, but today they are joining with them."

* A mother and father said: "This is the only time that we have been to a public event with our son that wasn't a courtroom."

* Mr Bob Gibson, the then Senior Governor of Prisons in Northern Ireland, said: "It's the most exciting programme of its kind I have ever seen."

* Mrs Briedge Gadd, Northern Ireland's Chief Probation Officer at that time said: "You must tell your story and let the world know you are leading the peace."

* Lady Jean Mayhew, wife of Sir Patrick Mayhew the then Secretary of State for Northern Ireland, often expressed her admiration for the programme in public meetings, on radio, and even at the highest level within government.

* Jean Kennedy Smith, the then US Ambassador to Ireland, invited our participants and staff to her residence in Dublin for a day.

* Liam Neeson, famous actor from Northern Ireland, made a donation to support our programmes.

* Tom Kumpf, from Bolder, Colorado, an American Vietnam Veteran, International Photojournalist and Author of *Children of Belfast*, said: "It's the only thing I've seen that works."

In 1996 Higher Force Challenge received recognition at an international conference on crime prevention. This was held in

Jerusalem and had been organised by senior rabbis. Out of over 100 submissions from across the world, three were accepted for presentation at the conference, one from Finland, one from the Philippines and ours. I had the privilege of travelling to Jerusalem, accompanying Mr Bob Gibson, mentioned above, as he conducted the presentation on our behalf. Beyond this, we entered the Allied Irish Bank's Better Ireland Awards in 1998, and out of many hundreds of applicants from across the island, Higher Force Challenge was the only programme within the youth category to make it to the grand final from Northern Ireland. Although we did not win, it was still a tremendous achievement.

A major article on Higher Force Challenge was included in the 1996 January edition of the Readers' Digest, and shortly afterwards, a full chapter was devoted to Higher Force Challenge in Steve Chalke's book, 'FaithWorks 2' published by Kingsway UK.

Chapter 6

The Risks are Real

Regardless of all the plaudits and positive recognition of the good we were doing, the risks were real. Young people are at risk because their environment is influenced and controlled by drug dealers on the one hand, and by paramilitaries on the other, although oftentimes these entities are one and the same! A significant number of young men have been victimised and assaulted by paramilitary organisations controlling their respective communities on either side of the divide. In the past young men were more likely to be shot in the legs or have their kneecaps blown off. In recent years, the shootings have been replaced by vicious attacks with paramilitaries wielding baseball bats and iron bars. These beatings resulted in injuries such as broken arms, broken legs, cracked ribs and fractured skulls.

I have visited many young men, both Catholic and Protestant, in hospital and at home, who were victims of such gruesome punishment attacks. One young man who frequented our centre had been shot in both elbows, both knees and both ankles, all sustained in the same attack. Another young man was called out from one of our sessions; taken away and shot in both legs. Another young man, who was a member of our staff, was told by his father that a taxi would pick him up at 9pm on a Friday night. He was to get into the taxi, which would take him to a meeting with a punishment squad who went on to shoot him in both legs.

Although he was due to work until 10pm that night, we knew we had to let him go early. It's hard to believe that, nowadays, this kind of summary punishment is still being inflicted by terrorist groups within Protestant communities.

The same can be said of Catholic communities where the IRA and other similar organisations have set themselves up as defenders of the people. In truth they have killed and maimed many within their own community. I visited a young Catholic man in hospital who had both arms and legs broken. He also sustained four broken ribs and a cracked skull. His attackers accused him of dealing drugs, but it was a lie. They were actually after his brother who kept eluding them, so they took him instead. In another punishment attack, the IRA attacked a young Catholic man in North Belfast in an incident that became known as 'the crucifixion'. Yes, they literally crucified him. They drove spikes through his hands and feet, pinning him to the ground. This was just part of their service in defence of their own community.

Even while writing this book, in 2015, a young man was beaten in his own home within our community by members of the UDA who, not content with beating him, nailed him to a worktop in his kitchen. Just a few weeks before this, members of the same UDA group pulled alongside a young man on the Shankill, jumped out of their cars and proceeded to beat him to the ground. With his body bloodied and broken, he managed to make it to our centre after 8pm. When members of our staff saw him, they immediately called an ambulance and the police. He was asked why he came to New Life City Church, to which he replied: "I knew it would be open and I knew I would be safe there."

While many manage to heal and get on with their lives, for others it may not be possible. When the IRA, in the New Lodge area of Belfast, shot one Catholic man in both legs, the perpetrators pulled out telephone wires so he could not call for help. This caused him to bleed to death. Likewise a Protestant man with three young children, living in the Glencairn area of Belfast, was shot in both legs by the UVF, and was also left to bleed to death. However, he was taken to hospital with enough time to save his life, although both of his legs had to be amputated above the knees.

Noel was a young man in his twenties from the Shankill Road in Belfast who frequented our centre almost daily. Noel had special needs. One day he never made it to the centre, because the UDA apprehended him. They dragged him into a nearby vacant flat where they tortured and executed him. When his body was discovered, it was found that he had been very badly beaten, suffered numerous lacerations and broken bones, before being shot in the head. Those responsible sought to justify their actions by branding him as an informer - someone who passed information to the police regarding the activities of a terrorist group.

The truth is, that young man was not an informer. His birth certificate may have indicated a 26-year-old, but his mind was that of a 12-year-old. Those who killed him knew this to be true, but it suited their cause to brand him in this way. The fear that this senseless murder instilled in our community resulted in very few people attending his funeral. Had IRA terrorists killed the young man, I can claim with confidence that thousands of Shankill Road people, including politicians and other dignitaries and community leaders, would have attended. Yet, to our shame not more than twenty attended the funeral of this young Shankill Road man. Some of those who killed him still live among us. Others fled to Scotland as a result of a feud within the UDA. They might have escaped justice here, like so many others, but someday – God will be their judge!

With all the violence, especially aimed at young men, am I as a pastor simply going to climb the steps to the safety of the church platform every Sunday to preach my next sermon? Or, I am going to step outside the safe place, get out of the system, speak up and speak out, and condemn the evil, whether inside or outside the church? The fact is - we must become responsible for those who are around us. It's time to stop playing Christianity and put down our spiritual soothers and time to be the church!

Chapter 7

The Dangers Increase

A date that is etched on the collective mind of the Shankill Community is October 23, 1993. It began as just another Saturday with people strolling along the Shankill Road doing their weekend shopping. Mothers pushing buggies, fathers taking children by their hands, wives holding on to their husband's arms, but for many of them, this day would change the rest of their lives. For some of them, their lives would end.

Unknown to the many unsuspecting shoppers that day, the IRA surveillance had gathered information that the room above a popular fish shop was used by UDA members. That day two IRA men carried a bomb into the crowded Frizzell's fish shop where parents and children queued to obtain some of the best fish in Belfast – Suddenly, the bomb exploded, killing one of the terrorists and seriously wounding the other. More to the point, nine innocent people were killed and several were severely maimed and injured.

At the precise moment the bomb exploded, we were in our centre facilitating training for youth and children's workers. We had just taken a break for lunch when suddenly our building literally shook. We heard a loud explosion, which was immediately followed by what sounded like a prolonged rumbling. We knew it was a bomb and that it was close by. We ran outside and could see that the bomb had exploded about 100 yards from us. Some of us immediately ran down towards the bomb site to offer whatever help we could. Many who were nearby and uninjured ran to the scene and immediately began to claw their way through the debris with bare hands; while others did what they could to help the injured. The police were on hand very quickly and were soon joined by other emergency services. It was like a war scene, and while we knew there were fatalities, it was not until later in the day we learned the full extent of the devastation in terms of lives lost, and of injuries.

As a local church minister and community leader I, along with others, were interviewed on television and radio about the bombing. During the interview I took the opportunity to condemn the IRA and its leadership for this attack on our community, and the cold-blooded murder of nine innocent people.

However, recognising that this indiscriminate bomb attack could lead to retaliation on the Catholic community I went on to say: "The people of the Shankill Road would have found it easier had it been terrorists who were killed rather than innocent people; not that we want to see anyone dead."

In hindsight this was perhaps not the wisest thing to say. I thought it was just a simple statement of fact, but unfortunately it was not seen that way by the local UDA leadership. My comments did not go down well with them at all. Soon I was contacted by someone who told me he had information that the UDA leadership had voted for me to be shot dead. He further told me that two of those present at the meeting, two brothers, had volunteered to carry out the shooting. He then advised me to seriously consider leaving Northern Ireland.

Knowing the leadership of the organisation, and knowing what they were capable of, I knew my life was in danger. I felt I had been misunderstood; that my words had been twisted. I felt betrayed by people within my own community, even though these particular people were terrorists. I felt threatened and I felt a sense of danger, but I refused to run.

Twenty minutes that saved my life

On the very night I received this information, I was meeting with members of our church evangelism team. I left home that evening around 7.20pm and arrived at our centre just moments before our meeting started at 7.30pm. None of the team was aware of any death threat against their pastor, but before leaving for home when the meeting had ended at 10.10pm, the leader of the evangelism team surprisingly asked: "Pastor, do you mind if we pray for you?" He spoke to the team and said: "I don't know what it is, but I really sense that some kind of danger is lurking, and that we need to pray for Jack's protection."

Knowing what others did not know, I was happy to receive that word and to receive prayer from the team. They gathered around me, laid hands on me, and began to pray. In fact they took time to pray. One by one they prayed. There were eight of them, and most of them prayed aloud. The result was that their prayers kept me there for an additional twenty minutes, and unknown to them, these were twenty minutes that saved my life!

When I finally made my way home, I drove slowly along my street, taking the time to look into parked cars and checking out the hedgerow, making sure that no one was in the vicinity. I slowly drove past my home, to the end of the street and back again. Confident that it was clear, I pulled the car into the driveway. No sooner had I entered my home and locked the door when someone started knocking. I quickly moved to the side of a window in my living room. Pulling back a curtain ever so slightly, I could see one of my neighbours standing at our front door. I had no idea why he was there.

Certain that he was on his own and that he posed no threat, I opened the door and brought him inside. He told me he had been watching two men who were hiding in the shell of an unfinished house which was being built opposite our home. He said: "Jack, I don't know what they were doing there, or what's going on. All I know is that for the past three hours (from 7.30pm to 10.30pm), they were watching your house as if they were waiting for you to come home." He then said: "They only left fifteen minutes ago, and I've been watching for you in case it's something you need to be aware of."

I thanked him for his concern, although I did not tell him what had been happening. After he left I reflected on the time of prayer with our evangelism team, and realised that the God we serve had intervened and had once again been looking out for me. I have often looked back to that night and wondered what might have happened if the team leader had not heard from God at that moment. What if he had not spoken up and offered to pray? What if I had not personally received that word and had not welcomed their prayer?

Often in my mind I have played out a different ending to that night of what might have been. In fact even today, several years later, when I walk from the car to my front door late at night, and when I'm putting the key in the lock of our front door, I still have mental images of what could have happened, but I'm thankful for the voice of God that speaks, and for the obedience to God's instructions as Solomon said: *"In all your ways submit to him, and he shall make your paths straight"* (Proverbs 3:6). However, while thankful, and whilst acknowledging the hand of God in all of this, I continued to take whatever precautions I could, but I also continued to remain active within the community, refusing to quit and refusing to run.

A few days later, the two brothers were arrested when caught with loaded weapons in their car, which indicated they were on a mission. They were several yards from our centre when they were stopped, and had been driving in our direction. Although I was in the office at the time, the police could not confirm that I had been the target. Facing the charge of having loaded firearms with intent, their older brother came and sat in my office and asked if I would write a letter to the judge requesting they be released on bail. I immediately laughed at the idea, but before I dismissed it, which I almost did, I distinctly sensed God saying to me: "Jack, use this as a bridge!" So I did.

Their older brother was also in the UDA and would have been one of the 16 that voted for my death, so how I responded to his request was critical. Writing letters to the court was not new to me. So I agreed. My letter was not only instrumental in the two brothers being released on bail, but it caused the judge to attach a condition to their bail, and that condition was that they should attend the next Higher Force Challenge programme at our centre. This was not what I had expected, but I nonetheless agreed to accept them as participants. However, two weeks prior to the start of the next session, the brothers were caught again, only this time with explosives in their car, resulting in them being sent to prison for several years. So we never did get to work with them.

Although I have never officially been informed that the death threat had ever been lifted, it is nonetheless my understanding that the decision had been taken to reverse it. Furthermore, on several occasions, in my capacity as a member of the Maze Prison Board of Visitors, I met with one of the most notorious commanders of the UDA, sometimes in his cell. Our meetings were always pleasant and friendly and that enabled me to realise that beneath every hard exterior there is a human being who would be so different if the circumstances were different. Somehow, I was never fooled by his pleasantries and in my heart I knew that this person was one that I could never trust, as William Shakespeare said: "Love all, but trust few." This guy was certainly not one of the few.

Facing death threats and avoiding assassination attempts was not what I had signed up for as a Christian or even as a pastor. I had signed up to attend church, sing a few songs, and preach sermons from my *safe place* within the building we call church, but not this. This was something I expected while in the UDR, but not as a pastor. Yet this was to become more and more part of who I was as a Christian and as a pastor. I was being drawn more and more into situations that were far removed from normal pastoral duties and normal church life. Where men with woolly faces (balaclavas), grenades strapped around their chests and guns held aloft, would be my audience, and sometimes my pursuers, from the day I decided to follow Christ, my life was no longer my own, but His. As Paul said: *"I have been crucified with Christ and I no longer live, but Christ lives in me. The life I live in the body, I live by faith in the Son of God, who loved me and gave himself for me"* (Galatians 2:20).

Chapter 8

Not Another Church!

Getting to the point of becoming the pastor of another church was not something that came easy for me. C H Spurgeon advised one of his students to go and do everything he could to prevent himself from going into the ministry, and that after having done so, if he still ended up in the ministry, he would then know it had to be God. Well I know that my Bible College days were over, but I have to say that I did everything I could to make sure I would not go back to pastoring, and yet it still happened. So here I was, even though I knew there were already 42 churches within our community, and being in agreement with the UVF member (a rare thing) who said the Shankill Road did not need another church. However, even though I believed that, I still ended up in this position of pastoring New Life, but I knew I was not doing this for me.

So how did I end up in this position that was now bringing me into the heart of community issues, not only as Director of a developing community project, but as Pastor of New Life Fellowship, later to become New Life City Church?

It really began in Jerusalem 12 months earlier. I was sitting on the lawn of a Jerusalem hotel in June 1992 speaking with Professor Mal Fletcher, from Australia, now living and ministering in Copenhagen, Denmark. As we talked about youth culture and the church's general failure to properly relate to contemporary youth,

I felt a burning desire to do something positive to help bridge the ever-widening gap between young people and the church. It was right then, sitting on that lawn that the Spirit of God spoke clearly to my heart and was clearly saying: "Go back home and start another church, but not another of the same, but one that would touch the lives of young people."

It was one of those moments when you just know that it's God. There's an inner conviction that will just not go away; a fire burning in your bones that nothing will quench; a 'must needs' moment when you feel a sense of destiny and excitement, and you cannot wait until you're back home to release what's inside. Knowing this was God, I was determined at that moment, that as soon as I returned home I would make an appropriate response. After weeks of much praying, my spiritual side, and feeding my concerned coffee-drinking side, I decided to launch New Life as a church that had a major leaning towards young people in terms of ministry and outreach. While we continue to grow, I believe we have not lost this focus.

The verse that God gave us for the launch of New Life was Isaiah 60.18 where God said: "You will call your walls Salvation and your gates Praise." We put this verse on all of our literature, even though we had no gates, and the only walls we had at that time were the outside walls of our building. However, the significance of this verse was to be revealed some 13 years afterwards with the purchase of a warehouse, explained in detail later.

During those formative years, while we were experiencing the blessing of God, we were also facing difficulties. I was becoming more and more outspoken of the paramilitary groups that maintained strangle holds on our community. During one of those difficult times, the president of the Elim churches in New Zealand, Pastor Bob Lawson, was speaking in an Elim Church in another part of Belfast. He had taken over from the previous president, Pastor Ian Bilby; a man I loved and greatly respected as a preacher. I thought that if Bob Lawson had stepped into the shoes of Ian

Bilby, he must be worth going to hear, but I had no idea what was about to happen.

The meeting had already commenced as I was shown to my seat. At the end of the service Bob invited pastors and other church leaders to come forward for prayer. This is not something I would always respond to just because the term pastor is used, yet that night I knew in my spirit that I needed to step forward for prayer. Bob Lawson began to pray for those at the front. He prayed for the person right next to me, and then it was my turn. However, during the course of his prayer for me he paused, and then prophesied the following:

"The Lord has heard the cry of your heart for the hill, and the Lord wants you to know that He is going to give you the hill."

At that time we were struggling to hold on to the old Stadium building. There were financial pressures, but there were also paramilitary pressures. One UVF commander was overheard saying: "When we get Jack McKee out, he's not getting back in." This was relating to the fact that we were having to sell the building, but were doing so with the promise of a new building in its place, and the promise that we would one day return as core tenants (although we never did).

However, shortly after the above prophecy, things started to take a different turn. Our bank manager phoned and offered us a shop unit opposite the old Stadium. All we had to do was to clear a small debt owed to the bank by the previous owner. This we were happy to do, thus taking ownership of our first building outside the old Stadium. Not long after this we were able to purchase another building above several shops on the Shankill Road and made the decision to move New Life and several of our activities to this new facility we named *Top House*.

Soon after this, we were offered vacant church premises at the lower end of the Shankill Road. The amazing thing is that this was my original home church where I had made my commitment to follow Christ as a teenager. This was also the church where Kathleen and I first met and where we were married. Now, shortly after the above prophecy, we had three other buildings outside the old Stadium. One was at the top of the Shankill, one in the middle, and the other at the bottom. It felt like God really was giving us the hill in the face of rising opposition from local paramilitary groups, although it should be noted that two of these buildings were not much to look at, but they were ours, and there was more to come.

Buildings change, but vision remains

In July 1998 we became tenants of another building; this was the new building that had been erected on the site of the Shankill bombing, where Frizzell's fish shop once stood. Here we opened a new outreach facility with a cafe we had named *Stars and Stripes*. Upstairs, there was a meeting and conference room, a games room, offices and a prayer room.

Eventually, we had to give up the old Stadium where we had started, back in 1989. It was an old building, in poor condition that required significant funds to put it right, but the funds were not forthcoming. However, buildings are just a means to an end, not our reason for being. We fully recognised then, as we still do today, that there's a danger in becoming building-focused as opposed to being people-focused, so that as we pray for the hill, we do not seek more buildings, but like the Son of Man, we seek the lost who are everywhere.

We chose to go into the heart of the community, creating opportunities to connect with the wider neighbourhood that would enable people to come to faith in Christ. Several of those we were able to reach out to, and who began to attend New Life, belonged to local paramilitary groups. They were faced with having to speak with their commanders to let them know they were now Christians and therefore it was no longer appropriate to be in the organisation. Normally, they were permitted to leave without any problems, although in some cases they would be forced to at least attend meetings and continue to pay weekly dues, or in some cases pay a substantial fee so they could walk away.

However, life would seldom become easy. Let me tell you about Joe. I first met Joe when he was sixteen. I visited him in prison. During that first meeting Joe committed his life to Christ. However, the next time I saw him was soon after he was released. He was at home with both of his legs in plaster casts. Members of one of the local paramilitary groups had blasted him through the back of the legs with a shotgun. I spent time with Joe encouraging him and praying with him. He began to attend New Life and became very much involved in the activities of the church and our outreach programmes. He was doing so well.

One night our phone rang; it was Joe's mother. She was somewhat distressed and asked if I would call to the house. Within minutes I was right there. I entered the home and there was Joe sitting with his head in his hands, while his young brother Jameson was sitting on the sofa with blood pouring from his head and face. They told me that Jameson had been beaten inside a taxi company, but whatever their reason, they had beaten Jameson quite badly, and now Joe knew he could not let this pass. He felt he had to avenge his young brother, and although Jameson and Joe were really close, Joe blamed Jameson for putting him into this situation where he felt he now had to put things right.

Nothing I could say would stop Joe from going off to do what he felt he had to do. Off he went into the darkness of the Shankill streets. My concern for Joe and what he might do, caused me to immediately gather some of our men at New Life who understood how these things worked. We searched for Joe by going to certain places and homes where he might have gone for obvious reasons.

Finally we found him and managed to talk him into a car. We got him back home, but the danger was far from over. We entered into talks with the paramilitary group responsible for beating Jameson, who finally assured us that as long Joe backed down, then he and Jameson would be left alone. While this was accepted and appreciated, we as a church believed that Joe needed some time and space to calm down. So we took up an offering and sent him, with my son Jonathan, to Colorado to stay with some friends in the Rocky Mountains. We believe that going to the USA at that time saved his life, but when he finally got back home, things continued to get worse rather than improve, not just for Joe, but more so and sadly for Jameson, as you'll read later.

Chapter 9

My Brother's Keeper

The fact I was now working as a pastor within our community, stemmed from the fact that when I was a young Christian, I was greatly influenced by books written by the late David Wilkerson, founder of *Teen Challenge*. One of those books, *The Cross and the Switchblade*, showed how he reached out to gang members in New York City. He did not sit back in the comfort zone of a religious nest blaming society for all that was wrong, and neither did he condemn the gang members or blame their environment or their family circumstances. He simply felt a sense of responsibility for a section of his nation's youth who were caught up in the cycle of despair and hopelessness, as expressed in drugs, crime and violence.

He wrote the story of a young man in a wheelchair who had been tragically beaten to death by members of a gang, wielding chains. What added to this tragedy was that while this young man was being beaten to death, and even as he was calling out for help, people living in the neighbourhood closed their window blinds and shutters and locked their front doors. No one came to his rescue. No one offered to help.

Upon reading this story, even though at that time I was still young in the faith, I determined in my heart that I would never ignore the plight of someone in need or in trouble. I decided I would never pull down the blinds or lock the door to anyone in need, but I had no idea that such determination would actually be put to the test. Soon I was confronted with the situation of a Catholic man in his teens, who, during the early days of the Troubles in 1971, had strayed into our community, and was being severely beaten by eight young men, also in their late teens and early twenties.

As they punched and kicked him, I could hear him scream for help. Fearing for his life, and not thinking about possible consequences, I pushed through the mob and threw myself on top of him. I remember shouting: "Go ahead, kick me as well." Thankfully they did not, although if given the same invitation today, some would gladly accept! I helped the young man to his feet and walked him through the mob, and continued walking with him until he was safely out of the neighbourhood. This was the first of many that God gave me a chance to help over the years, even to this present day.

More often than not, it's been young men we've been called upon to help, who for various reasons have come under threat from local paramilitary groups. In fact we have even helped several paramilitary members who themselves had fallen out of favour with their organisation. We have never turned anyone away. If someone came to us for help we would do our best to do whatever was appropriate to help resolve the problem, which at times had the potential for serious consequences, and all this while directing community outreach programmes and pastoring a church.

One of the more serious and most dangerous acts of intervention, and there have been several, was back in 1995 when I received a phone call from a young man in his twenties. He very nervously told me he was calling from a secret address in England and that his name was Martin McGartland.

A British agent in the IRA...

I had heard of Martin McGartland, but I had never spoken with him or worked with him prior to this phone call. In fact, I was quite surprised he was calling me. Martin is from the Catholic community on the other side of the dividing wall in Belfast, but had been living in hiding in England for many years from the IRA. As a young man he had worked for the Police Special Branch in Northern Ireland, involved in intelligence and information gathering, or as some would say an informer, which for any paramilitary group was lowest of the low. He explained to me how the IRA had badly beaten, mutilated, and shot a number of his close friends, with one of them being shot on several occasions, and how that this resulted in him looking to get back at the IRA in some way.

The information he had gathered and passed on to Special Branch was quite productive, leading to the failure of several IRA operations and the saving of many lives. In fact he was so good, that the police eventually convinced him to infiltrate the IRA and work as an undercover agent. He quickly became one of the top undercover British agents in Northern Ireland. Through his help the security forces uncovered many weapons and explosives belonging to the IRA, but more to the point, he was instrumental in the saving of over 50 potential IRA murder victims.

His cover, as a British agent had finally been blown, resulting in him being tortured and interrogated by the IRA. Before they had a chance to execute him, he managed to escape by jumping through a third-storey window, which left him in a coma and critically ill. It was after surviving this attempt on his life, coupled with the fact that his cover had been blown, he moved to England and obtained a new identity.

However, as a result of the injuries he sustained in jumping through the window, he was in the process of claiming for damages, but there was a problem. He told me the courts will not permit his case to be heard in England, so he had to appear in person in a Northern Ireland courtroom, which could put his life at great risk, because the police had refused to provide protection for him. The fact is, the Special Branch did not like the fact that Martin had written his first book, *Fifty Dead Men Walking*, which resulted in one of the police officers telling him, he was on his own.

Martin asked if I could do something to encourage the relevant powers in Northern Ireland to provide him with the necessary protection. I knew without doubt that this was a very dangerous scenario for me, or for anyone else to get involved in, but I knew I could not be selective after vowing to help those in need – I certainly was not expecting this one! This would test me to the limit; for not only would the IRA be extremely unhappy with anyone who helped Martin McGartland, but so too would the paramilitary groups within my own community, who I'd already angered several times.

While Martin referred to himself as a British agent, as did others, the paramilitaries on both sides saw him as nothing more than a tout, an informer. Yet I knew, regardless of the realities and the dangers, that if I closed the blinds and pulled down the shutters and locked the door on him, my philosophy of helping people would be struck a fatal blow. Besides, what would Jesus do?

However, I did not agree to do anything on his behalf until I was satisfied that he really did save lives. I asked him for details of people he claimed were saved so I could confirm with them the truth of his claims. He was happy to provide some names and dates, and so I spent the next week following up on these. This was good for my prayer life as it caused me to seek God for guidance, wisdom, and protection. I had no idea where this would lead, but I knew that Christ was leading from the front. I had already committed myself to following Christ, and rather than just sing *Where He May Lead Me I Will Go*, I was willing to get out there and go. In doing so, I met with four people who all confirmed they had been approached by the police who had told them they had received intelligence showing they were being set up to be murdered by the IRA. This was enough to confirm to me that Martin was legitimate, and so on that basis I agreed to do what I could to help.

The first thing I did was to make contact with the then Secretary of State for Northern Ireland, Sir Patrick Mayhew, and then with the chief constable of the police in Northern Ireland. I explained that a Martin McGartland would be attending court in Lisburn, on October 7, 1996, and that on his behalf I was requesting that appropriate security be provided to ensure his safe passage from Belfast International Airport to the courthouse. I insisted that such security should remain in place throughout the day and until he was returned to the airport after the court hearing. I further made it clear that if this was not forthcoming, then a number of our church members and centre staff would be willing to travel with Martin in convoy and stay with him throughout the day, providing the authorities with an even greater security problem than having to look after one person.

Soon I received a call from a senior police officer letting me know that my request had been granted, and that security would be provided on the relevant day. From that moment on I was to have no contact with anyone, other than one officer until the day of the hearing. One week prior to the court hearing, police officers drove me to the airport to meet with the airport police. Step by step they took us through the measures that would be put into place on the day Martin would arrive at the airport. It seemed that everyone was now taking this extremely seriously.

On the day of the hearing I was again picked up by police officers around 6am. There were two cars with armed plain-clothes police officers in each. When we arrived at the airport we drove through security gates where we transferred to an airport police car. From there, we drove out to the tarmac where we sat and waited for the plane to arrive from England.

I finally got to meet Martin in person as he was first to exit the plane. We got into the police car and drove straight to the court. Driving along the country roads, we noticed how seriously the authorities had taken this. At every junction and roundabout, police officers were standing alongside police motorcycles or cars. They waved to the officers in the car as we passed. Their presence gave us a sense of security, and put us all at ease.

Order in the courtroom

We got to the court around 8am by which time police officers had already surrounded the courthouse, which was beside an army barracks. This reassured us. We entered the courthouse believing it would all be over in a few hours, but we were wrong. The judge decided he would hear every other case before hearing from Martin. We spent the entire day sitting in a small room, drinking coffee and eating sandwiches, until we were finally called around 4pm. We had no idea what was about to happen.

Shortly after Martin took the witness stand, the entire courtroom violently shook in response to a large explosion. Police officers ran from the courtroom while Martin grabbed hold of the witness box, fear clearly etched on his face as he looked over to where I was sitting, seemingly wondering what was happening and what he should do. The judge looked towards the police officers who were still in the room as if looking for instructions. I mean what do you do when you're a judge and a terrorist bomb has just rocked your courtroom?

The tension in the courtroom was so intense. No one knew exactly where the bomb had exploded. We knew it was nearby and wondered if the courthouse was the actual target. The judge regained control of the courtroom, while Martin began again to answer questions, only this time quite nervously; not helped by the fact that the barrister asking the questions was just as nervous. But why be nervous? The bomb had exploded and we were all still in one piece. No need to be nervous, or so we thought.

Not more than five minutes after the bomb had exploded, the courtroom shook for a second time as another bomb exploded. The police soon reported to the judge that two bombs had gone off in the army barracks right next to the courthouse, with the second bomb causing serious injuries and taking life. One has to ask, why this day and why this time, and why this place? It was no coincidence that it was at the very time that we sat in the courtroom, and the very moment that Martin was standing in the witness box, that the IRA chose to detonate two bombs right next to us, leaving over thirty injured and a warrant officer dead.

The judge brought the case to a much quicker conclusion, stating he sympathised with Martin and would love to be in the position of awarding him damages, but that the law prevented him from doing so, because regardless of his reason for joining the IRA, or as Martin would say, 'infiltrating the IRA', the fact remained that Martin had been a signed up member of a terrorist organisation at the time of his injury. The judge explained that his hands were legally tied in this case, and ruled that Martin should not be awarded injury claims. Immediately after the hearing, we were quickly removed from the courtroom and driven at high speed through the streets with blue lights flashing and sirens sounding as we made our way back to the airport. It had been a long day. Martin was put back on the plane, while I was dropped off at home. We were still alive, at least for the moment.

Chapter 10

Shot and Left for Dead

Martin McGartland continued to stay in touch by phone, I got one of his calls on June 14, 1999. It was a Monday morning and we chatted for about five minutes, which was fine, then he called back the following day, and then again on Wednesday. It was strange for him to call me three days in a row. However, when he called on the Wednesday, he told me he believed the IRA was closing in on him. He said he believed it was only a matter of time before they would finally shoot him. I did my best to calm him down. "The IRA is on another ceasefire," I said. "The IRA has signed up to the Good Friday Agreement. They've decommissioned their weapons," I said. "And it was witnessed and confirmed by several independent observers, chaired by Canadian Military General John De Chastelain."

However, Martin McGartland knew different. He knew what was going on around him much better than I and others did.

The very next day I was listening to the news and to my horror I heard it reported that Martin McGartland had been shot that morning in England. I was shocked. He had been shot six times. Early that morning he had got into his car, but as he tried to close the door he felt it being held open. Next he knew, a gunman was pointing a weapon towards his head. Somehow he managed to grab hold of the gun and pull it downwards, directing it away from his head, but the gunman pulled the trigger over and over again hitting Martin several times in the chest.

Riddled by five bullets and his thumb hanging off, Martin believed he was dying. The gunman fled the scene believing he had finally finished off one of the top British agents in Northern Ireland. Neighbours arrived on the scene, and Martin was taken to hospital to undergo major surgery. He survived the attack, which he believes was carried out by the IRA. Yet in spite of this attempted murder, and other successful executions at that time, the British and Irish governments stated that the IRA ceasefire was still intact. The then Secretary of State for Northern Ireland, the late Mo Mowlam, speaking on behalf of government, referred to this, and to other shootings and murders, as 'internal housekeeping matters'.

Martin has written two books, *Fifty Dead Men Walking* and *Dead Man Running*. The former is also the title of a film that is based on the book, although he would say the film is very loosely based on his book. He remains in hiding, and continues daily to look over his shoulder, knowing that those who want him dead are only a step or two behind. I could have done without him in my life. I had a church to run, services to plan, and people waiting on me to call for a coffee, but sometimes we just need to put the coffee cup down, and go where the need and the Spirit of God takes us.

Chapter 11

Terrorist Death Threat

Soon after this, as Martin McGartland moved on as best as he could with his life, and as I remained focused on reaching out with the Gospel across our community, a one-time member of the UVF, who had fallen out of favour with the group, began to attend New Life City Church. He became very active and helpful in the church and the outreach, even travelling to the USA and becoming involved in churches with us there. He owned two flower shops, and after being with us for some time, he told me the UVF demanded he pay protection money. I had no reason not to believe him, as protection racketeering is one of the ongoing past-times of most, if not all, paramilitary groups. I began to speak out via the media against the UVF on his behalf, which led to some very heavy and dangerous discussions with members of the UVF who told me that this man was leading me on, but I chose to believe him rather than them. After all, he was a Christian, and they were not.

Tempers were raging, and I was often quite sternly asked: "Who do you think you are?" A question often asked by those who believe that their ability to terrorize gives them the right to question everyone else's legitimacy. Soon I found myself invited to meet with someone I trusted and to meet this person in a car, alone. It was made clear to me that I was treading on very thin ice and that certain members of the UVF were unhappy with my public comments. I was strongly advised to back off. I continued to speak out when I felt it necessary to do so, especially when, soon after this meeting, one of the two flower shops was totally destroyed by masked men wielding baseball bats.

So, regardless of what others were saying about him, a member of our church had suffered the destruction of his business. I was his pastor. What was I to do? Go and preach my next sermon and ignore what had happened? Not me! There I was, standing amid the devastation speaking to the local media. It was then that a member of the UVF brigade staff visited me in my office in the old Stadium. He left me in no doubt what would happen if I continued to speak out against the UVF.

I sat and listened to him tell me that they were about to give the order for me to be shot. At that moment I distinctly remember looking right into his eyes and, mentioning his name, I said: "You need to know three things - firstly, you need to know that I do not want to die, for I still have a life to live and things to do, and I'm not speaking out like this so you could come and threaten me like this."

"Secondly," I said, "you need to know that I do not fear death, because I'm ready to die, and because I know where I am going." But then I said: "Thirdly, if you do choose to have me killed, then the God I serve is the God you will stand before someday and you will be accountable." He replied by saying, "I believe in God too you know!" which opened the door for another brief debate before he finally left, slamming the office door behind him.

This left me feeling very uneasy and deeply concerned. However, I continued to believe it was important to speak out, and I did so, which brought further threats and warnings. This time the warnings came through people who were 'in the know', people who I knew and trusted who were expressing serious concern for my safety. In fact, they frightened me more than the person who came to my office, because they were sharing what they were hearing from friends within the UVF.

So feeling threatened again, and believing in my freedom to speak out and in the freedom of a community to stand up for itself, I decided to do something I had never done before. I decided to contact the ministers of our local churches within the Shankill community. It was time to 'call them out' and encourage them to come together to stand against this death threat. After all, I would do it for them! So I approached several church leaders within our community, letting them know of recent threats and asking them for help and support. The response I got was frightening, and even embarrassing to write about.

One local minister showed no reluctance in making it clear to me that he did not want to get involved. Another was unavailable, so I explained the situation to his wife and stressed the urgency of the moment, requesting that he call me as soon as possible. He never did get back to me. It was one brick wall after another, but my disappointment was to be greatly increased when I spoke with a minister I had greatly respected at that time, as did many others.

Told to run...

I could only get speaking with him on the phone, and when I explained what had been happening, he quickly told me it was not the church's responsibility to stand up and speak out on these matters. What? Was I hearing him right? Was this a man I had respected within our community? He went on to say: "Jack, all this business about taking your stand is not Biblical." I felt like David must have felt when he was being patronised and demeaned by his older brother Eliab and was waiting on him saying: "With whom have you left your few sheep?" I responded by saying: "Are you serious? What about the Old Testament prophets who spoke out against injustices in their day?" I then said: "What about John the Baptist and even Jesus who stood up and spoke out against those who were using and abusing the people? Were they not taking a stand for righteousness and a stand against evil in their day?"

There was more to come, because not even attempting to

answer my questions he continued by saying: "Jack, perhaps you should consider doing what Jacob did when threatened by Esau."

Wow! I was shocked to say the least, and now with emotion in my voice I responded by saying: "Are you kidding me? Are you suggesting that just as Jacob chose to leave his home and go off to a far country until Esau's heart had changed, that I should do the same?" He said: "Well perhaps until things quieten down." Wow again!

I could hardly believe what I was hearing, especially coming from this particular person, but I clearly heard what he said. My final words to him were to express my disappointment and to say: "I don't see myself as a David, but if I have to walk onto that battlefield and face the giant alone, and then look back and see men like you still hiding in the trench, then so be it." I concluded by saying: "I'm not being ignorant here, but I'm going to hang up now, and I don't think you and I will be speaking again." Neither we did. Sometime after this he left the area.

In the meantime, the UVF, through another source, made it clear they were not responsible for what had happened at the flower shop, and that furthermore they would not be approaching the owner again for any donations. I had no reason to doubt what they were saying; in fact I was starting to believe them. So I passed this on to my friend, the flower shop owner, thinking it was what he wanted to hear, but boy was I ever wrong.

Instead of appreciating all that had been done, including the risks taken by me and also by others, he accused me of being weak and of capitulating to terrorists. Well I ask you: "Do pastors get angry?" I did! This drew such an angry response from me, "How dare you!" I said, "I have literally put my life on the line for you." Maybe I should have gone and preached that sermon! Maybe I should have had that cup of coffee with wee Lizzie and prayed for her bunions. Maybe I should have stayed and looked after those few sheep. I could not understand what was going on in his head, but this was the beginning of a rift between us, but worse was to come, much worse.

Chapter 12

My Sister's Keeper

It was at that time I received a call from a Catholic woman from East Belfast. In a distressed voice she said, "Are you the wee (meaning short) Pastor who's on television?" She told me that her son had been beaten up and put out of his home and that two female members of the IRA had also beaten his 19-year-old girlfriend, a young Catholic who was told not to contact the police, but to remain in her flat until IRA men came to take her away. If she had already been beaten, why would IRA men want to take her away? Where would they take her? What would they do with her? Would she be seen again, or would she simply be one of the Disappeared? The several men and women from Catholic communities killed by the IRA and buried in fields - some remaining missing for up to 45 years or never found at all.

The woman on the phone was distraught, and I had no idea what I could do. I asked her: "How long do you think we have before they call for her?" She replied: "I don't know. I just know they said they would be there soon." The thought of contacting the police was out of the question. It would not only be pointless, but also dangerous for the young woman. I was able to call the young woman and speak with her on the phone. She was so frightened. I knew someone had to do something and quickly, but who was that someone? There was no someone - I was that person!

She nervously explained to me that she had been told that IRA men would arrive at her home within thirty minutes. Realising I only had twenty minutes to respond, and that I could be at her home in about ten minutes, I suggested that the only thing I could do was to drive to her home and remove her from that situation, hoping to get there before the IRA arrived, and then hoping to negotiate her safe return to her home at a later stage.

Knowing how dangerous this was, and that I had to ensure my own safety and that of anyone else who chose to go with me, I called a senior police officer; someone I had known quite well and could trust. I quickly explained I would be driving into the Short Strand area of East Belfast for the single purpose of driving this young woman away from immediate danger. I told him I would be covering the license plate on my car so that no one could easily identify me. I made it clear that my only reason for contacting him was to make him aware of what was happening in case something went wrong. I asked for an assurance that no police officers would be in the immediate vicinity while I was there, because the presence of them would make the IRA believe it was the young woman who had contacted them. He gave me this assurance, and said he would pass this to units on the ground.

So with two others, Willie who was attending New Life at that time, and Elizabeth, my sister-in-law, who was the manager of our café at the centre, I drove across the city with my number plates blackened out. When we got to the Short Strand area, I stopped to check there were no police patrols or suspicious looking people in the neighbourhood. Seeing the streets were clear, we drove cautiously to the home of the young woman where we stopped and scanned the streets one more time. Believing the way was clear and that no one was around, we stepped out of the car and began walking towards the front door. We had barely taken a few steps when suddenly, we were surrounded by eight police officers, all pointing guns at us. A sergeant placed the barrel of a machine gun about four inches from my head. As he did so he screamed at me: "Get down on the ground!" I refused.

Screaming back at him I shouted: "I'm a Pastor from the Shankill Road." That was enough to let him know I was in a dangerous place. I continued shouting; "This woman's life is in danger and I'm here to take her out of here, but you guys have blown it!" All the while he's screaming back at me while peering over the barrel of his machine gun and ordering me to the ground. Still refusing I shouted: "Contact Tennant Street (a police station), they should have let you know I'd be here." Meanwhile, Willie was likewise being challenged and responding in kind, but Elizabeth could be heard screaming from the back seat of the car all the way back to West Belfast! A police officer pulled open the car door and pointed a gun directly at her, ordering her to get out, but she just sat and screamed.

All of this happened within just a few minutes, but then just as suddenly as they had arrived, the police patrol was ordered to withdraw immediately and leave us. Within moments they were gone. However, what had become a hive of activity and noise for some five minutes had now become eerily quiet, although there was one main difference; the streets were not empty anymore. Startled and bewildered small clusters of neighbours had gathered outside their homes, including a group of four men standing watching our every move. The police were gone, and we were now on our own. Feeling quite vulnerable, I yelled at the girl we had come for, who by this time was standing at her front door, to grab what she could and get into the car. Within moments we were in the car and driving away from there, with the young woman safely in the back seat alongside Elizabeth, who at this point was in no fit state to be of any help to anyone.

Thirty minutes later I received a phone call from a member of Sinn Fein (political wing of the IRA) within the Short Strand, from where we had taken the girl. He spoke to me by name saying: "Jack, where have you taken her?" I said; "What makes you think that I've taken the girl?" He said: "We know it was you, because someone in the street recognised you." I responded by saying: "Well my only concern is for the safety of the young woman. All I want is to help resolve the matter and to have her returned safely to her own home as soon as possible." This led to discussions that eventually resolved the situation with no further threats or injuries, and with the young woman eventually returning safely to her home in the Short Strand.

However, when we removed the young woman from her home, we put her in a 'safe house' and placed her boyfriend, who we had also managed to rescue, in the home of the man who owned the flower shop, who had offered to help. But then without consulting with me, or with those who had taken the young woman into their home, the flower shop man took it upon himself to take her from the other home and bring her to his house. Even though our relationship was already under pressure, as soon as I heard what had happened I spoke with him and told him he was out of order. He said nothing, but just stood staring at me with glazed eyes and a quivering lip. From that moment, he never returned to New Life, but the rift between us was to get much wider.

Chapter 13

The Writing on the Wall

Many of the walls within our community are covered with murals or graffiti. We were fortunate at the centre, because although we were right on the front of the road and had a whole lot of exposed wall around our building, generally we escaped the attention of the would-be graffiti artists. However, when we turned up at the centre one morning, the word 'ICHABOD' had been spray painted across our front wall. This is an ancient Hebrew word that appears in the Bible and means *'The Glory has departed'* (1 Samuel 4:21). Not many people would be familiar with this biblical word, but someone was! They even knew how to spell it, but who could it be? We decided at that moment to ignore it and to simply paint over it.

To our surprise, the next morning it was back. There it was again in large capital letters, ICHABOD. We then decided to contact the police when we learned that one of their night patrols had already taken note of the graffiti. They had in fact written ICHABOD into a notebook and were trying to figure out what the letters stood for. They thought it might be some new terrorist organisation. We laughed at the humorous side of this, but still wanted to get to the bottom of it. We explained to the police that ICHABOD was in fact a biblical word, and shared with them its true meaning. However, we were still at a loss concerning the identity and intent of the phantom graffiti writer.

Once again we painted over it, but the next day – it was back - ICHABOD, in bold spray painted lettering. Three mornings in a row! It was now apparent, that someone was trying tell us something; that someone was going out of his or her way to make a point, but who was it? Some of our staff volunteered to stay up and keep watch through the night to see if they could catch the phantom ICHABOD writer, but there was no guarantee they would come back for a fourth time. Surely not?

Well, at 3am, a car pulled up at the front of our building, and to everyone's surprise, stepping out of the car was the flower shop man. He had a can of spray paint in his hand. Glancing up and down the road and satisfied it was clear, he walked towards the Stadium wall. Giving the can one last shake he was about to spray its contents onto our stone canvas when our staff members challenged him. Caught red-handed, his first reaction was to just stand there looking at everyone. He was like someone being awakened from a deep sleep, and in a daze, he just walked back to his car and drove off. The police were immediately informed and although he was caught, we chose not to press charges.

I know it's not for us to judge, and that we should leave the final judgment with God, but Jesus did say concerning those who are true Christians: *"By their fruit you will recognize them"* (Matthew 7:16). Not by their spray cans, but by their fruit! Even Gandhi said: "I like your Christ, but I do not like your Christians, because your Christians are so unlike your Christ." So this completed the rift between us, but I had bigger things to face - I had a God-given vision to pursue, and I knew there was more to be done in the city.

ICHABOD never appeared again, but the flower shop man was far from finished. While I tried to re-focus on pastoral duties and on moving the church forward in its ministry and outreach, he chose to go down a whole different road.

He finally ended up in prison on a 15 year sentence for having a primed bomb and a loaded weapon in his car with intent to endanger life – not ours, someone else's. On his release from prison he returned to the Shankill Road, but was finally threatened and expelled from the community by the UVF, because he was trying to throw his weight about.

While all this was going on, I received a phone call one afternoon from the UVF brigade staff member who had come to my office – mentioned in Chapter 11. He told me he needed to speak with me. Not wanting to be seen to be jumping to his 'request' I told him I would not be able to meet with him for a few days. Soon after I put the phone down I decided to call him back and told him I'd be with him in fifteen minutes, because I now wanted to know what was on his mind.

Before leaving home I told Kathleen where I was going and who I was going to meet. This was something I seldom did, but I needed her to know.

I said to her: "If I don't call you in an hour, I want you to phone the police and tell them where I am." Once again Kathleen was left wondering what was happening and if she'd have to make that call. Soon, I was pulling up in the car outside the offices of the UVF on the Shankill Road. Before going inside I walked around my car several times pretending to check my doors were locked, but wanting to make sure that people saw me going inside.

While making my way into the building I was saying to myself I hope he doesn't bring me into the *backroom*. I'd heard so many stories about '*the backroom*' and they were not good. As I entered the reception area, there he was, three others were also there. I knew one of them, who likewise was high ranking within the UVF, and I recognised another. There was no mutual greeting, just a few quick glances. He immediately invited me into '*the backroom*'! I reluctantly followed him while the others remained outside. The 'backroom' was nothing but an office with a desk and some chairs. I'm sure the walls had ears and if they could talk I'm sure they would have much to say. My main hope at that time was that I would not be adding to anything the walls had witnessed previously.

As we sat on opposite sides of the desk I noticed a copy of my first book *Through Terror and Adversity* sitting on the desk.

When I asked him what this was about he lifted the book and said: "It's about this."

He said: "We've read your book and believe it's all made up and is nothing but lies."

I responded by saying: "That's my book and those are my stories and every story in that book is true, but is there one in particular that you have a problem with?"

He said: "Well yes. You write about a member of the UVF brigade staff going to your office and threatening to have you shot."

He went on to say: "Every brigade staff member has read this and they all say it wasn't them, so your story is lies, and the men want to know who it was that went to your office."

Now there I was, sitting looking across the desk at the very person who was in my office, and he was telling me the story was made up! So what am I supposed to say or do? Well, I can tell you that I did pray and that my prayer was just as brief as Peter's prayer when he was walking on water, but took his eyes off Jesus and focused on the waves and began to sink. At that moment Peter cried out and prayed one of the shortest prayers ever: "Lord save me." So as I sat there I was internally crying out: "Help me Jesus."

I looked into his eyes and I said: "Listen! There are only three who know the truth of this."

I said: "I know it's true. The person who came into my office knows it's true, and God knows it's true, and I'm happy to leave it at that."

At that point I stood up and told him I was leaving. He immediately got off his seat, walked round to where I was standing and shook my hand as he opened the door. I walked past those who were still sitting outside and left for home before Kathleen made that call. I have no idea what he said to those waiting outside or to any of the other brigade staff members.

Sometime after this he became ill and sent for me. I visited him in his home at least once a month over the last year of his life. At times I was on my knees on his living room floor, laying hands upon him and praying for his healing and for his salvation. Tears would often flow down his face as he told me of his belief in God, but also of his inability to serve Him because of his commitment to the UVF. It is my hope (and belief) that in his own way he did make his peace with God. It is not for us to judge, but to reach out and to minister to people regardless of who they are or where they live.

Praying for all

I pray for the salvation of all, including terrorists. One of the church's greatest leaders, Paul the Apostle, made it clear that although we are involved in an ongoing conflict: *"Our struggle is not against flesh and blood"* (Ephesians 6:12). Our conflict is against negative spiritual forces in high places; against demonic influences and against the devil himself who is the prince of the power of the air, and is the god of this present world, whose power is finite and whose days are numbered.

In 2 Corinthians 10:3-4 Paul wrote the following: *"For though we live in the world, we do not wage war as the world does. The weapons we fight with are not the weapons of the world. On the contrary, they have divine power to demolish strongholds."* The greatness of our faith is not that for which we are willing to kill, but that for which we are willing to live even to the point of death, first and foremost the death of the soul, that is the death of self, and if ever called upon as have some, the death of the body.

True obedience to Christ does not result in hatred for those who oppose us, but in our ability and willingness to love even those who are our enemies.

Jesus taught us to love our enemies, that is, to desire their highest good, and to pray for those who hate and abuse us. He was not a leader in word only, but a leader in action and example. When He died, He died not only for His friends, but also for His enemies as Paul wrote *"while we were God's enemies, we were reconciled to him through the death of his Son"* (Romans 5:10). I am also most effective as a Christian not when I reach my friend with the message of Christ, but when I reach my enemy, and so I reach out with the belief that my enemy might one day become my friend and my brother in Christ, which has often been the case.

Chapter 14

The Enemy's Camp

Praying for the enemy from a distance is easy; loving the enemy from a distance is not so easy, but is possible. As a young Christian I can remember gustily singing: *"I went to the enemy's camp and I took back what he stole from me. He's under my feet, Satan is under my feet."* It was a great song that got the feet going, and by that I mean tapping the feet along with the beat of the music, but that was it. There was plenty of singing with gusto, but not much going into any camp, and the only thing under my feet at that time was a pair of soles with holes in them, but I had no idea that years later I would be literally living out that song.

Someone derogatorily said: "The devil lives on the Shankill Road!" My response was to say: "Well, if that's true, then there is no better place for the church to be than on the Shankill Road!" We believe that God has called us to set up camp in the heart of the devil's territory, but not with a besieged mentality, for God has enabled us on numerous occasions to enlarge the place of our tent, to spread out to the right and to the left, and without fear. We do so knowing it was Jesus who said that he would build his church regardless of any enemy, physical or spiritual. He said: *"I will build my church, and the gates of Hades will not overcome it"* (Matthew 16.18).

So against this background, and against the backdrop of narrow-minded criticism from within certain sections of the church, and blatant opposition from certain sections of the community, New Life City Church continues to reach out and to touch those who are hurting. We continue to be the hand of Christ, extended to a hurting and wounded community.

We refuse to become the type of church that was tragically symbolised by a certain American minister as he was leading a prisoner to the death chamber by walking in front of him. As the prisoner was taken from his cell for the last time with chained hands and feet, he walked awkwardly behind the chaplain, a church minister, who led him along 'Death Row' to the place of execution. The minister walked with his back to the prisoner, and was reading verses from the Bible as he approached the electric chair.

At one point, the prisoner spoke up to ask the minister a question. He said: "Sir, do you really believe what you are reading?" The minister turned to him and said: "Yes, of course I believe." The prisoner responded by saying: "Sir, if I believed even half of those things, I would crawl on my hands and knees across this earth, and on glass if necessary, to save a single soul." The minister proceeded to turn his back on the prisoner, and began once again to fulfil his religious duties by continuing to read the scriptures as he escorted the prisoner to his death and into eternity.

What a sad and pathetic image that reflects a church mechanically fulfilling its religious duties while the world is going to hell in a basket.

I have watched The Patriot several times, a movie about the American War of Independence starring Mel Gibson as Benjamin Martin and Heath Ledger as his son, Gabriel Martin. In one scene he rides up to a church to gather fighting support from the men inside. As he approached the church, he stopped for a moment next to a tree where three men were hanging by the neck. As Gabriel sat on his horse, looking at the men, he could hear the singing of a hymn coming from the church just a few yards away. I'm sure it wasn't 'I've been to the enemy's camp', but they were singing in the safety of the church building, and the pastor was getting ready to preach his next sermon, while three men had been hanged just outside the door just because their skin colour was different! And I wonder at times, what's changed?

Regardless of paramilitary activity and of people like the flower shop man, we had determined as a church that we would not be caught up in the performance of religious duties while those around us were dying and while many were blindly marching towards a lost eternity. We determined that those living within our community would not see us as a *drive-by-church*, driving through the community on our way to our place of worship and then driving back for Sunday dinner, but that as much as possible and however possible, we would connect with those living within our streets.

I don't know about you, but I am not content with living in a religious comfort zone. The church was never intended to be one of the biggest or one of the wealthiest organisations on earth, but was created a living organism to provide answers to the suffering and death that surrounds it; to be a life-giving force, infused and energised by the Spirit of the living and life-giving God. Jesus was the giver of life who improved the quality of life for many, while he extended the duration of life for others by healings and resurrections, and gave eternal life to those who believed in Him.

He did not confine himself to the preaching of sermons, but he fed the hungry, and gave water to those who were thirsty, and he did so without forcing those in need to listen to a sermon before they could eat or drink. He healed those who were sick and brought deliverance to those who were oppressed or possessed. He said: "*I am the way and the truth and the life. No one comes to the Father except through me*" (John 14:6), and He further said: "*I have come that they may have life, and have it to the full*" (John 10:10).

Chapter 15

Changing Our Image

The conflict in Northern Ireland has projected such a negative image that needs to be challenged and changed. The positive side of Northern Ireland life has been waiting for its moment to burst onto the international stage. There is a different story to be told.

There are more Titanics to come out of Belfast (built in Belfast, but you do realise that we didn't sink it!) There are more George Bests waiting to contribute to the international football scene, although I'm not sure if we can ever discover eleven that could bring us back a trophy or two. More snooker champions like Dennis Taylor and Alex Higgins waiting to be discovered at the end of a cue. More boxing champions like Wayne McCullough and Barry McGuigan ready to step into the ring and fight it out glove on glove. More international golf champions like Rory McIlroy. More successful Formula One drivers like Eddie Irvine. More motorcycle heroes like Joey Dunlop. More entertainers like Van Morrison and Snow Patrol who can thrill the world with music and song. More writers like C.S. Lewis, Jonathan Swift, Seamus Heaney, Oscar Wilde, Samuel Beckett and of course the Bronte sisters, to name a few, who can captivate the imaginations of children and adults alike. More world-renowned actors like Liam Neeson and Kenneth Branagh who can rise to stardom without forgetting their roots.

There are more with the pioneer spirit who would dare to blaze a trail of human advancement, rather than the fire of destruction, and more who are still foolish enough to believe that the Bible contains a life changing and world-changing message, and willing to boldly travel from these shores to far off lands to proclaim and promote faith, hope and love through a message that is old, yet ever new.

In my lifetime, I have witnessed first-hand a nation that has turned in on itself, destroying over 3,700 of its children and some of its visitors. I hear the blood of our fellow islanders, of men, women and children, call out from the ground, calling for a just and lasting end to the madness that has dominated our blood-stained history. Yet I also see the rise of a different spirit within a new generation of young people who are refusing to wear yesteryear's cloak of sectarianism and bigotry.

Sadly, I can also see that there are those among us who refuse to move toward a better future. I see those who have chosen to remain stuck in the quagmire of sectarianism, refusing to step up and step forward to embrace a collective freedom where all would benefit. I see those who would rather live with the divisions of the past than to embrace the unity, or even the diversity, of respect and tolerance for all. I see also a church that has all too often become part of Northern Ireland's troubled past, whether through constant negative and sometimes bigoted statements, or even through its deafening silence rather than giving the lead towards a positive and just solution.

I thank God for those who have not only refused to be silenced by the intimidation of paramilitaries, but have refused to be constrained by the tradition of the Pharisees and the trappings of dead religion. I thank God for those who have discovered the truth of a vibrant relationship with a living and life-giving Saviour, and are bold enough to believe that God is going to do a *new thing* in our day. I thank God for those lives that have been transformed by the power of God, victims and victimisers alike, who stand together in worship, with no thought of retaliation or vengeance. I thank God for those who have been forgiven much, for they love much and desire to do much in return. I thank God for the cloud of witnesses that will rise above mere religiosity and who will proclaim a message of Christian love and Godly freedom for all, for: *"If the Son sets you free, you will be free indeed"* (John 8:36).

We claim to be a Christian nation, yet so many fail to understand that being Christian is not simply a matter of culture or even doctrine, but it's who you are in Christ, reflected in what you do and in how you live. In other words, Christianity is not just a set of beliefs, but a lifestyle. It is not just saying: "I believe in Jesus," but it's actually following Jesus. Paul the apostle, quoting the prophet Habakkuk said: *"The righteous will live by faith"* (Romans 1:17). This is why Paul also wrote: *"For it is by grace you have been saved, through faith, and this is not from yourselves, it is the gift of God - not by works, so that no one can boast"* (Ephesians 2:8-9). James however, took us beyond the point of conversion to discipleship when he wrote: *"Show me your faith without doing anything, and I will show you my faith by what I do"* (James 2:18 NCV). The fact is, the Christian faith finds expression in Christian works, even to the point of becoming all things to all men that we might by all means save some (see 1 Corinthians 9:19-22).

When we look at the condition of any nation, and not just Northern Ireland, God does not say: "If the politicians…" He does not say, "If the paramilitaries…" He does not say: "If the people in the community…" but He does clearly say: *"If my people, who are called by my name, will humble themselves and pray and seek my face and turn from their wicked ways, then will I hear from heaven, and will forgive their sin and will heal their land"* (2 Chronicles 7:14). So if any nation is not experiencing wholeness and wellbeing, it is not solely down to the terrorists among us, or to crooked politicians who rule us rather than serve us, but God clearly places the responsibility of this at the feet of His people, the church.

God still asks the question: *"Whom shall I send? And who will go for us?"* (Isaiah 6:8), and he's looking for the same response he got from the prophet Isaiah who said: *"Here am I. Send me!"* Let's not look to others to solve the problems of our nation, but let's look to ourselves; let's look to ourselves as believers to be the church. While we should hold politicians to account, it's time we stopped looking to government offices for a word, but let's look for the word that's needed to come through the church, for what matters is not who's in the White House or who's in the doghouse, but what matters is who's in God's house, and who's prepared to take the word from God's house to the highways and the byways that are outside the church, not inside.

Despite all we have gone through, with the pain and destruction of decades of violence, hope is still alive and well among many of us. We may not have magic forests with fairies flying through the trees, or little leprechauns sitting at the end of the rainbow on a pot of gold, but we do still have hope and aspirations for a better future for all. My plea to those in other nations, especially in America, who claim to be *friends of Ireland,* is that you ensure that your contribution to Ireland will actually assist in our advancement, and not in our demise. Too many within Belfast and across Northern Ireland, have died at the hands of their fellow Ulsterman or Irishman, and it wasn't always the enemy on the other side.

Chapter 16

Brother against Brother

If ever Psalm 91 had any real significance for me personally, and for those we work and enjoy fellowship with, it was surely during the year 2000. The year had started well. It also started with millennium fever, and despite the Y2K predictions it brought with it a new sense of hope and expectation. However, no one foresaw the darkness that would descend upon our community before the year would end; a darkness that was both physical and spiritual; a darkness that would destroy lives and homes; a darkness that would turn neighbour against neighbour, and even worse a darkness that would turn brother against brother. This darkness was referred to as the loyalist feud, Protestant paramilitaries fighting against and killing each other.

It was during this period that the first eight verses of Psalm 91 took on a role of immediate significance for New Life City Church. God was telling us that we would dwell in the shelter of the Most High; that we would rest in the shadow of the Almighty, and would not fear the terror of the night nor the arrow (bullet) that flies by day. We had no idea that a new fear would soon grip our entire community.

Saturday, August 19 was the beginning of the bloody feud between the UVF and the UDA, and before that weekend was over, three men ended up dead after being shot. Seven others had been shot and seriously wounded; some families were thrown into sudden and unexpected grief, while dozens were violently evicted from their homes and from the community where they had lived for many years. Fear gripped the entire area as the violence between these two very powerful and heavily armed organisations was so viciously unleashed.

The fear that gripped our community was unlike anything we had previously experienced. We were used to the violence imposed upon us by the enemy from without, which had the tendency of uniting people, but what was happening now, through this internal feud, was tearing the community apart, and was ripping the very heart out of families.

This not only presented the community with a challenge, but I felt the church, and more specifically New Life City Church, needed to respond by at least trying to do something to help bring peace to a very difficult and dangerous situation. I was not just a pastor responsible for a church, but this was my community; this was my home turf; this is where God had planted us, and many of our individuals and families were living right in the midst of this madness. I quickly found myself back on the streets, visiting church members, friends and family members, some of whom had been directly affected by this sudden outburst of violence.

While sitting in one such home I received a call from someone who told me another young man had just been shot dead in the Oldpark area of Belfast, an area adjacent to the Shankill. The young man in his twenties had been shot and killed while visiting his girlfriend. Soon the phone rang again. This time it was to let me know that a woman within our community had suffered a heart attack, due to the fact that her husband had been threatened with death if they did not get out of their home. I immediately left and went to the hospital. I spent a few moments talking with the woman and then prayed with her before leaving at 1.30am.

As I left the hospital, after such a long and tragic night, I felt passionately that someone should speak out to at least try to do something to help bring an end to the feud. So I took it upon myself to call BBC Radio Ulster. They interviewed me right away and played the recording at 2am and then on the hour, every hour through the night and then again at breakfast the following morning. During the interview I called on all church ministers and church leaders within our community to meet with me to discuss a united church response to the downward spiralling situation. I had no idea how they might respond, especially after my previous experience, but this was not a private discussion at the manse door or on the phone, this was prime time radio.

That morning at 10am, a total of twenty church leaders turned up, but that was only the start. From this meeting, we put out a joint press release calling for an end to the violence. Several of us, as local ministers standing together, also appeared on a number of live television and radio shows. We called on Christian people within our community to join us for united prayer at the Methodist Church. More than 200 responded by coming together for two hours of prayer. This prayer event was also given good press coverage that helped show that the church was stepping up and was at least trying to do something. Thankfully, after several months, the feud ended, but, seven had died, dozens had been wounded, and hundreds evicted from their homes. Our community had been damaged from within.

Chapter 17

New Life City Church Steps Up

As a church we have often taken our stand against terrorism, drug dealing and racketeering across the community, and beyond. During the weeks and months of the feud we felt motivated to identify with the community. We felt compelled to create our own response to the tragedy that was literally tearing our people apart. Some of the things we did, besides calling on churches to step up, were as follows:

1) To organise a *peace march* along the Shankill Road calling on the UVF and the UDA to end their violence.

2) To organise our own *March of Witness* through the streets of the Lower Shankill.

3) To turn our youth hall into a *furniture store* to house furniture belonging to some of those who had been evicted from their homes.

4) To physically help people move from their homes under the cover of darkness and under the watchful eye of armed police officers and soldiers.

5) To prayerfully walk the streets for three hours every night during the feud, meeting and talking with frightened residents, but also with members of the UVF and the UDA who were on duty at almost every street corner.

We touched the heart of the community and touched the lives of many as we walked and prayed and spent time connecting with people, encouraging them to hold on and to believe in better days ahead. We also met up with British soldiers who patrolled the streets at that time. They had been instructed by their commanding officer to watch out for the New Life teams. They approached us in the dark and let us know that if we ever got into any difficulty we could call on any of their units on patrol, but thankfully we never needed their help as we were received well by almost everyone within the community. Our hiding place and our resting place was not the British army, but was under the shadow of the Almighty (Psalm 91).

We thank God for those who stepped up and stood alongside us during those days and nights, but while the feud was going on, we faced other tragedies. We had just finished an eight-week personal development programme with ten at-risk young men from within the Shankill community. The programme is called *Higher Force Challenge (HFC)*. Our staff had spent eight weeks working with these young men, supervising physical and non-physical group activities. The day after completing the programme, four of our young men were involved in a fatal car accident; one of them was sadly killed, while three others were seriously injured.

We thank God for the opportunity to touch a community through prayer gatherings and prayer walks, but are also thankful for the opportunity to work with young men like these, and similarly with young women, who face many challenges in a city where there are few solutions. We can only hope and pray that our influence on these young and impressionable lives will bring positive results, and that they will know that no matter how often they mess up we will always be there for them - not to condemn, but to help them move forward by making positive choices.

At that time, while driving through County Antrim in Northern Ireland, I noticed the remains of an old tree. It had obviously been dead for some time. All that remained was a stump, but what really caught my attention was the sight of a young sapling growing out

of the centre of the dead stump. It immediately reminded me of
the words of Jesus: *"Unless a kernel of wheat falls to the ground and
dies, it remains only a single seed. But if it dies, it produces many
seeds"* (John 12:24). So we thank God that in the midst of death there
is life, and on a personal note, I thank God that in the midst of our
community there is New Life, which will offer hope and courage as
we endure the feud and pray for it to end.

Chapter 18

Lifting Up The Cross

Danger, violence and death are words that are foremost in people's minds in a world that appears to be getting more violent and more dangerous by the day. I am by no means a pacifist, but I believe that our greatest challenge is not to react to circumstances according to the flesh, but rather according to the leading of the Spirit of God who has the power to change circumstances and to change lives.

Jesus called upon us to follow Him, and the only thing He told us to take up in our pursuit of Him is a cross. Of course He was not referring to a literal cross, but He was speaking of a life of self-denial, even to the point of being dead to self, yet there is something powerful that happens in the heavens and in the atmosphere around us when we actually take up the cross and carry it as a symbol of peace and reconciliation. I had never seen myself as a *cross walker*, one who carries a cross through streets and across cities, yet this was to become a significant part of my life and ministry as a result of the on-going violence in Northern Ireland.

It was during the above loyalist feud that I put out a call for a united peace march along the full length of the Shankill Road. The purpose was to mobilize Christians and non-Christians alike in a public challenge to call on the organisations to end the violence that was tearing the community apart. It was my hope that church ministers and leaders who were supporting the initiative would lead the march, but while all the plans were being put in place there were rumours that the UDA was planning to disrupt the march.

There was a clear sense of apprehension among some of our own people and among others who had planned to walk with us. Some were expressing concerns as they repeated some of the rumours they were hearing, that the UDA in one part of the community was planning to prevent us from reaching the bottom of the Shankill Road. At that point, as I remembered the words of Paul: *"For God did not give us a spirit of timidity (fear A.V.), but one of power, love and self-discipline"* (2 Timothy 1:7 ISV), I felt God brought a personal challenge to my heart concerning the need to motivate and inspire others. I knew I had to do something.

However, what was needed was more than words; it was something more tangible. Those who were planning to walk needed something that would help motivate and strengthen their faith. So the day before the planned march, I chose to walk along the middle of the road, following the white line from the top to the bottom of the Shankill Road, and to do so while carrying a 6ft wooden cross, holding it high so it was clearly seen. This was my way of saying: "Come on, you can do this!"

This was not something I had done before, nor had I thought I would ever do again. This was never part of my consideration in ministry; it was weird even thinking about it. Yet the sense of weirdness in a strange way became part of the confirmation that it had to be God, because very often the craziest ideas come from God. My natural man would never have considered such a thing. So as far as I was concerned this was the only time I would do such a walk.

I knew I was no Arthur Blessitt, a man of God from the USA who has walked the streets of hundreds of cities across the entire world while carrying a cross. He was one of those men who had left an imprint on my life as a young Christian that remained in the background for 30 years. It was in 1971, the first time he had walked with the cross outside of America, he walked right by me in Northumberland Street, where our church is located today. As he passed by, just a few feet from where I was standing, our eyes met as he walked from the Protestant Shankill to the Catholic Falls while carrying a large cross on his shoulder. He passed through a line of British soldiers who stepped aside, making an opening, to permit him to walk through to the Catholic side of Northumberland Street. I have not forgotten that image to this day.

So with Arthur Blessitt being my inspiration, even 30 years later, I headed off to do a *cross walk* in the hope of inspiring and encouraging others. Kathleen drove me to the Woodvale Park at the top end of the Shankill Road. Finding an appropriate place to stop, she left me off and quickly drove away, leaving me standing there with a 6ft cross in my hands. Talk about feeling nervous!

Not really alone

Standing alone, and feeling somewhat exposed, I felt a real sense of God's presence. I had this amazing feeling that just like Elisha and his servant, I was not really alone. So, taking a deep breath of the Shankill Road's fresh air, I lifted up the cross and rested the bottom of it on the buckle of my belt. I then moved to the middle of the road and just began walking, following the white line in the middle of the road, with traffic coming at me from both directions.

Many immediately responded. Motorists sounded their car horns in approval. Some rolled down their windows and spoke out to encourage me saying: "Well done Jack." Women stood at the edge of the pavement, some quietly looking on with sympathetic expressions on their faces that seemed to be saying: "We're with you Jack," while others called out and shouted: "Well done Jack." Others actually applauded, some with smoke rising from their hands as they held on to the cigarettes that were firmly fixed between their fingers.

As I continued walking along the middle of the road I saw several soldiers with two police officers patrolling the area. I thought for sure they would confront me and order me off the road, as I had not asked permission to do this. I began to rehearse in my mind what I might say if they approached me, and I wondered if I might even be arrested. As we passed by each other, my eyes looked nervously towards them when thankfully one of the police officers smiled at me and gave me a nod of approval. This was a reassuring sign that confirmed I was not going to be stopped or arrested for carrying the cross in such a manner.

The strangest moment, in terms of how I felt, came as I walked past the Rex Bar where the feud had actually started. It was a warm Friday afternoon, which meant that many of the men, who would normally be inside the bar drinking, were standing outside enjoying the sun, but even more-so, enjoying the beer. As I walked past the bar, I saw some of the men take a few steps towards the road. Holding their pint-sized beer glasses in their hands, they stood in silence and looked on as I walked past with the cross. None of them spoke; they just watched. Some I guess would have been thinking: "Well done," but not willing to say it out loud, while others would have been thinking: "What an idiot!"

As I walked towards the lower end of Shankill Road I began to feel a little more apprehensive, but this feeling soon lifted when three women stopped at the edge of the footpath. They applauded, and one said to me: "Well done Jack!" This did not make me feel any sense of self-importance, but was a welcome and timely word of encouragement. Several minutes later I was finally at the bottom end of the road. I had completed my first ever *cross walk*, and did so under very difficult circumstances. It did not matter what others thought or what they had said, or would say, about me personally. What mattered was that my attempt to encourage and inspire others was not confined to mere words or to the inside of a church building, but was public and transparent.

The following day, we were encouraged by the fact that more

than 500 people turned up for the march down the Shankill Road. Given the circumstances, this was a fair turnout. I was delighted when a number of local church ministers and other leaders stepped up and led from the front, but just ahead of them was one of our own young men, Jamie, who proudly led the way while carrying the same cross that I had carried the day before. The march was well-received by others within the community as many stood along the way and applauded as an expression of their support.

Once again as we passed the Rex Bar, I noticed some of the men standing silently, again with pints of beer in their hands. They looked on as we made our way past, but nothing was said. Soon we crossed over to the lower end of the Shankill where some of us had quietly expected that at this point we might receive some abuse, but thankfully this was not forthcoming. Afterwards, we were told that some of the UDA commanders in that area had told their people to stay indoors until the march had passed.

We finally concluded the march at the bottom with a brief word of prayer and thanksgiving led by one of the Shankill ministers. We prayed for an end to the ongoing violence that had gripped our community, and prayed for those who had already suffered during those tragic days, particularly for those families who had lost loved ones.

Words are great at times, as is preaching, but Isaiah said, *"How beautiful on the mountains are the feet of those who bring good news"* (Isaiah 52:7). We will never know the full extent of what was accomplished that day, but we do know that the people had been given an opportunity to speak out, and we thank God that many did. Churches had been given an opportunity to come together in a worthwhile, common cause, and we thank God that several did. The cross was lifted above the gun in the midst of a bloody feud and as a public challenge to those behind the violence to desist. We do not know everything, but we do know we did something.

Thank God that because of the lead given by those churches that had rallied together during those days of prayer and witness, along with the efforts of others within our community, the violence finally subsided. I pay tribute to all who made a positive contribution in helping to find a way forward at that time. Sadly however, the feud managed to spread to North Belfast where others were to likewise die before it eventually came to an end, but end it did.

Chapter 19

One Day Becomes Forty

I never thought I would ever lift the cross again in such a manner. Carrying the cross for one day was quite enough for me in terms of white line evangelism, but God had different ideas! Later, while sitting in Colorado, God presented me with a fresh challenge to once again carry the cross, only this time it would not be for one day only, but for 40 days, and it would not only be along the Shankill Road, my home community, but along the neighbouring Catholic Falls Road, running parallel to the Shankill Road, on the other side of the dividing wall.

I have faced many challenges over the years, and have responded well to most of them, but this was the most frightening of all. This was my Red Sea experience, yet I knew that for every Red Sea there is a way through and a way forward. This was to be my Jericho experience, as I would walk around the dividing wall in Belfast, and would do so alone, not for one day or for seven days, but for 40 days.

In the words of a well-known Christian songwriter, Don Moen: *"God will make a way, where there seems to be no way. He works in ways we cannot see, He will make a way for me. He will be my guide, draw me closely to His side. With love and strength for each new day, He will make a way. God will make a way."*

God had firmly planted in my heart the idea of literally carrying the cross around the streets of Belfast for 40 days, in such a way that it would focus the attention of the people, on the greatest historical and religious symbol in world history – the cross. The concrete wall that literally stands between our communities is a symbol of division and hatred, but the cross is a symbol of reconciliation and love.

Many offered to walk alongside me, but in the context of Northern Ireland this would have turned it into a procession, raising all kinds of implications, but would also have taken the focus off the cross. This was something I had to do alone, although Dennis from New Life would follow alongside on the pavement each day. The challenge to both communities was to look to the cross rather than look to the gun, but also to challenge the church to keep its focus on the cross. However, I had no idea what kind of reception I would receive in either community, especially on the Catholic side, as I would be simply seen as a Protestant minister from the other side of the dividing wall. I was therefore ready for anything!

One man with one cross

While making final preparations I realised I had not informed the police of my plans. I had talked to God about it. I had talked to Kathleen about it. I had talked to friends about it. I had talked to the church about it, but I had not talked to the police about it. So I made contact with the police station, just four days before the commencement of the walk. The police officer took note of my 'strange request' and said he would respond before the end of the day. What he did not tell me was that my request had to be placed before the Northern Ireland Parades Commission, but there was a problem. The members of the Parades Commission were all in South Africa.

So unknown to me the police actually made contact with the

Parades Commission in South Africa, who quickly put it on their agenda and then finally responded to the police in Belfast stating that 'one man carrying a cross along the centre of the road did not constitute a march!' It was therefore put back to the police in Belfast for them to make a response on the basis of personal and road safety issues. The police were finally willing to approve the *cross walk* along the middle of the road providing I used wisdom, took responsibility for my own safety and that of the motorists who might well panic seeing some guy walking towards them carrying a cross. Given that people in these communities had learned to live with someone coming at them with an AK47, I was certain that someone walking towards them with a 7ft cross would be a refreshing sight!

It was Monday February 18, 2002 when I commenced the *cross walk*. For the next 40 days, for 90 minutes to two hours each day, I would carry the cross with John 3:16 emblazoned across the front. I would follow a route through our divided communities and around the physical wall that stands as a concrete symbol of that division. I would face bewilderment, encouragement, discouragement, threats, applause, jeers, shouts of: "Away back to where you came from," and questions such as: "Why are you doing that?" and "What's that - John 3:16?" One young Catholic lad thought I had my name on the cross and shouted, "Hey John! What are ya doin'?" I think one of the funniest comments was when I heard one elderly lady saying to another: "Why doesn't he go and get himself a job?"

During those 40 days, besides the variety of attitudes, some good and some not so good, I would also experience the changing face of Northern Ireland's weather conditions, sweating when the sun came out, wrapping up when the winds were howling, wearing the wetsuit when the heavens opened, and looking like a walking snowman during blizzards. The full story of the *cross walk* has been recorded in my book *The Cross and the Gun*, but let me share some memorable highlights.

It was the end of the first week of the walk, and although the pubs are officially closed on Sundays in Northern Ireland, I was amazed to see men knocking on the front or the side doors of some pubs as I walked along the Falls Road. Soon the locked doors were opened and in they would go with the doors being quickly closed behind them. As I passed one of these pubs, several men, about five or six of them, came out and came running after me.

I could hear them shouting, and knew they were shouting at me. From the corner of my eye I could see one of them running towards me. I looked around, expecting to get a pint of Guinness on the side of the head. Standing next to me however was a young man in his mid-twenties. As I looked at him, I was still unsure what to expect. I wondered what he was up to, and was surprised when he said: "Well done mate, keep it up!" I can tell you, this did not only encourage me, but it caused me to breathe a welcome sigh of relief! They knew where I was from, but were delighted with what I was doing.

But it was not just the men in the pub, because not to be outdone, a Catholic nun came out from behind the gates of a religious building on the Falls Road. She came right onto the centre of the road and stopped me in my tracks, because she wanted to greet me. With a huge smile on her face she took my hand and said: "Thanks for doing what you are doing. We all think it's great, and may God bless you for this." She then invited me into the building for some tea, but I graciously declined, as I could not afford to drink too much fluid while walking. We wished each other well, and I continued with the walk.

Things were going so well at times that at one point I had to remind myself that Jesus said: *"Woe to you when everyone speaks well of you"* (Luke 6:26), which made me think that if the *cross walk* really was making an impact, then the response would not simply be positive, but in fact a hornet's nest would be stirred, not that I was looking for one! However, something was about to stir.

A car pulled out of a shopping area within the Falls Road with four men on board. The driver yelled out: "Hey Jack! How's Marty doing?" Taken by surprise I did not know who he was talking about, but then he shouted, "Tell that 'so-and-so' the IRA have not gone away." It was then it dawned on me, he was talking about Martin McGartland. He laughed and drove off while I continued with my walk. This unsettled me, because I left in no doubt that some within this community knew me better than I realised. But who were they? Who was he? I had no idea who they were, but I was left in no doubt as to who they represented.

Immediately following this, as if that wasn't enough for one day, two men came walking by. One of them looked at me with such hatred blazing from his eyes that he looked demonic. Then with anger in his voice he sneered and screamed at me, "Away back to the Shankill ya Protestant 'so-and-so'!" I looked straight into his devilish eyes and said: "God bless you my friend." He repeated the above and I responded by saying: "God bless you." He repeated the comment about seven times, with the same hate-filled intensity, but my response was always, "God bless you."

It looked like he wanted to come onto the road and rip the cross from out of my hands, or perhaps it was my head he wanted to rip from off my shoulders. However, it was obvious there was something stopping him from taking action against me, and I'm not simply talking about the Holy Spirit, who no doubt was working in my favour at that time, but it was also quite apparent with each passing day that *Mr Demon Eyes*, and others like him, were under orders not to harm me - as much as he and others may have wanted to.

Diabolos was about to show up!

Then there was St. Patrick's Day. I had assumed that anyone carrying a cross on St Patrick's Day anywhere in Northern Ireland would be welcomed as a saint. There I was, carrying a cross and walking past the St Patrick's Day revellers, all of whom were sporting green and white and drinking Guinness. As I approached where they were standing, some of them began to laugh. They were laughing at me, the man with the cross. One young woman, wearing her St. Patrick's Day t-shirt, shouted out: "Hey mister, you're a header." (meaning an idiot). I then thought to myself at that very moment: 'How sad that on St Patrick's Day in Ireland, the man who carries a cross is the one considered to be a header!' It made me wonder what they truly thought of Patrick. However, this was just the hornet's nest being stirred; Diabolos (Greek for the devil – the accuser) was about to show up.

Three men made their way into the middle of the road, with one of them leaning right into my face. This was escalating into a very serious and threatening confrontation. During the confrontation it became quite apparent that he was in charge of 'the turf' where I'd been walking with the cross. It soon became obvious that the person who confronted me was in fact a commander of the IRA in that area. However, his problem was not so much with me walking with the cross, but was due to the fact that two others were walking with me on the footpath handing out little cards explaining what I was doing. The atmosphere became extremely tense as he threatened to punch the heads off those with me.

As he was breathing out his threats, using his extensive range of expletives, another man who had greeted us on a previous day saw what was happening and came to our assistance, but before he could say a word, the local IRA commander quickly turned on him and said, "If you open your 'so-and-so' mouth I'll dig the 'so-and-so' head off you." Knowing who he was dealing with, our Good Samaritan friend froze on the spot, which sent us a clear signal regarding the position and the power that this person actually had within that community.

The situation was seriously getting out of hand, when suddenly another man appeared in the centre of the road with the intention of getting involved. He did not have the look of a deliverer. In fact I was frightened for him. I looked at the man. I then looked at the one who had just joined in, and I thought to myself: "If he opens his mouth, this guy will kill him." But no! It was the very opposite! In fact it soon became clear that the man who had just joined us was superior in rank to the man who had been spewing out threats, and moments later it was all over. The bully went back to the high-rise flats he had come from, while I continued walking the other way with the cross, once again lifted high until we safely got back to the other side of the wall. Yet even there it was not always that welcoming or safe.

While walking along the middle of the Shankill Road, I noticed a white car driving straight at me – I mean – it was literally coming straight at me. There were four men in the car. Those I could see clearly were rough-looking characters. In fact they were ugly, especially the driver. I could see the car coming towards me, but I held my ground and my nerve. My only response was to slow up, but I continued to stay on the white line in the middle of the road even though the car kept coming towards me.

As the car was almost right on me, the driver swerved away at the last moment! He screwed his face up at me and was mouthing expletives while the others, including one young lad in the car, just laughed. He was making the point that he and some others were not happy with what I was doing on the Shankill Road, not so much with the cross, but by my very presence in the Shankill community. Our paths were to cross several other times beyond this point, but never pleasantly.

I recognised the driver as one of the local commanders of the UDA 'C' Coy who controlled the Lower Shankill, although a major power shift was to occur during the next 12 months; a power shift that would cause him and other local commanders to flee from the very community he and they had controlled for years; in fact, they had to flee Belfast altogether, moving to England and Scotland, as detailed later in this book. However, I prayed for the driver, that he and his friends would be around each time I walked with the cross daily without fear on my part, and that the sight of the cross would become etched on his mind and the minds of his friends.

This prayer was answered! One full year later, as we were taking part in a late night prayer walk through the streets, a young man stopped me and said: "Hey Jackie, do you remember when you carried the cross on the Shankill last year?" I said: "Yes, why are you asking?" And with a huge smile on his face he said: "My Da tried to knock you down!" His father had fled to England at that time, but not before he and his brother put bricks through the windows of my car and my son Jonathan's car at the front of our home, because I had prevented them from shooting a man at the back of a filling station on the Shankill Road. This was another situation where the cross in my hand was lifted above the gun in theirs.

Chapter 20

One More Challenge

The 40 Day *cross walk* was almost complete, and I was so looking forward to it being over. I wanted nothing more than just to finish and go home. In fact, I had a deeper understanding of Forrest Gump when he said: "I think I'll go home now!" But before I could do so, God had another plan for me. It was day 39 when I knew that God had directed me to go to the Sinn Fein office on the Falls Road to present them with a gift. This was a major step on my part as this office was a representation of those who had been responsible for many deaths within the Shankill community, including some of my friends, and who I believed had made at least two attempts on my own life; carried out a failed bomb attempt and a failed shooting bid.

But part of my background was equally a representation to them of the violence, which they believed had been inflicted on them by the Protestant community and by the British. So I had enough reason not to go anywhere near their office and they had enough reason to not let me in. Yet I knew that God had showed me so clearly that it was not enough to simply walk past these offices sporting a 7ft cross, but that I needed to show I was willing to reach out to those who were the perceived enemies of the community I was from. This had to be God. If not, I was in trouble!

When I got to the front of the building the doors were locked and a camera was pointing down in my direction. I pushed a buzzer and waited for the door to open. When it did, to my surprise, it was the man who had previously come to our rescue the day Diabolos came out to challenge us, who greeted me at the door. He immediately recognised me. Calling me 'Pastor Jack' he welcomed me with a friendly and hearty handshake. I handed him a mahogany framed mirror that had a Celtic cross on it, but also had the entire words of John 3:16 printed on the mirror in the Irish language. He gladly took it from me, but that wasn't enough for him. Oh no! I was not getting away that easily.

He proceeded to invite me inside to show me around the offices and to introduce me to those who were inside. On another day this never would have been happening for either of us, but it was happening on this day. Unable to just turn and walk away, I responded to his invitation and went inside to have a guided tour. Those who were inside the offices received me well, as my host introduced me as 'The minister from the Shankill who's carrying the cross.' Before leaving, I expressed my sincere appreciation to the people on the Falls Road for putting up with me during the 40 days of the *cross walk*, because I knew I could not have done so without their approval, and in some cases, their tolerance.

I often wondered what happened to the mirror, and then nine years later, in 2011, Sinn Fein published a new manifesto that they placed in homes across Ireland and Northern Ireland. On page seven of the manifesto there is a photograph of several very prominent members of Sinn Fein sitting around a table inside one of those offices, and right there on the wall behind them is the mirror with John 3:16. At the bottom of the mirror is what looks like little prayer cards stuck between the glass and the frame. I am delighted to know that my mirror with the cross and with John 3:16 made it to the Sinn Fein manifesto.

It is my constant prayer that Christians everywhere will respond to the ongoing challenge to take up the cross and that they will genuinely follow Christ wherever he leads. Not so much to take up a cross made of wood, but one that is evidenced in our lifestyle and in our daily walk before God and men, and that more than anything we will continue to lift the message of love above the message of hatred; the message of reconciliation above the message of division, and the message of the cross above the message of the gun.

I wish I could say that the sound of the gun was never heard again in Belfast and that its fatal consequences are now behind us, but it saddens me that this is not the case even to this day. The sound of the gun can still be heard in Belfast and beyond, in spite of the fact that a peace agreement was signed in 1998 by politicians and by combatants on both sides of the conflict. It is an agreement that's been changed several times and broken many times with murders that have not been considered a breach of the agreement, but in some instances have been labelled by politicians as *housekeeping matters*. However, no matter how many times agreements and ceasefires are broken, the cross continues to be lifted above the gun. Yet more tests were to come.

Chapter 21

Another Internal Feud

Just six months after the 40 Day *cross walk*, the guns were out again within the Shankill community, leading to further death and destruction. One woman spoke with me and said: "Jack, you don't know how much you impacted the paramilitaries on the Shankill Road when you carried that cross." She told me how she had heard several positive comments about the *cross walk*, even from paramilitary members. This was such an encouragement, to know that six months after the *cross walk* had ended, it was still being talked about, and that while the gun was once again being fired in anger, the cross was being remembered.

The UDA leadership had expelled one of their Senior Brigadiers, who was one of the leading terrorists within Northern Ireland. He was commander of the infamous and oftentimes ruthless C/Company, based within our community. Many of us wondered what it would mean for the Lower Shankill where the Brigadier and many of his close associates lived, and where his headquarters was based. We did not have to wait for long, because very soon the lid was lifted off, and more deaths were being recorded, including the assassination of another Brigadier who had been shot by members of the Lower Shankill UDA. Another Brigadier was shot through the face in a similar assassination bid. He survived that attempt, but not the second. Pressure was mounting against C/Company and against the Lower Shankill. Shots were being fired; blast bombs were being thrown; people were being killed, while others were hospitalised.

Once again we felt as a church that it was not enough to simply conduct services in the midst of violence, injury and death, but that we needed to respond more openly to the situation. We called the church to prayer immediately following our Sunday evening service; not just to *say prayers*, but to seek God's face on behalf of the community and to seek direction as to what we should do in helping to bring this new feud to an end. As we prayed, sang and worshipped together, one by one, people would come up to the microphone and pray for the community. Some would write on pieces of paper what they believed God was saying to them and to the church. It was during that time of prayer we felt that God had given us clear direction concerning what our response should be to the ongoing situation that would once again put us, as a church, onto the streets of Belfast and into a very precarious situation.

There was no time to waste. Our community was in turmoil. People were facing eviction from their homes and the threat of death. The following day I went alone to meet the Brigadier in question, who was surrounded by four of his men.

He received me quite well and instructed one of his men to make me a coffee. I talked with him about the ongoing situation and how tragic it was that lives were again being lost. He was quite sure as to where the responsibility lay for the feud and clearly pointed the finger of blame at the main UDA leadership. However, there was no regret or acceptance of responsibility on his part for recent deaths and shootings.

I then took the opportunity to share with him and his associates what I believed God's perspective was on all of this, and told them that New Life City Church was praying for them and for the community. They seemed somewhat stunned and were even speechless as I talked to them about God. They were much more comfortable talking about politics or about the feud than they were at talking about God. Yet nonetheless I had their focus. I believe God also had their attention in those moments and that in the midst of the violence, men of the gun were listening to a man of the cross, albeit out of courtesy.

However, the violence continued into the New Year of 2003, when other members of the UDA attacked the home of the rebelling Brigadier. He was later arrested for directing acts of terror. He was once again imprisoned until January 2005, but was still well able to conduct his operations from inside. As the violence increased, and more deaths were reported, we decided it was not enough to meet within the church building for prayer, but that we needed to take the prayer to the streets. Once again we were on the darkened streets doing prayer walks through the area controlled by the UDA's C/Company.

The tension was incredible. A number of men approached us in the darkness, but when they recognised us, helped by the armbands sporting a cross, one of them grudgingly grunted: "Hi." We returned the greeting, only without the grunt, and walked on. Within moments there were more men, but it was the same routine as before. There were six of us on that first night of the prayer walk; we divided into two teams of three. This is how it would be for most of the nights during the following four weeks. We walked in prayer through the snow, sometimes blizzard-like, leaving our footprints as we walked and prayed from 9pm through to midnight each night.

Meeting with Paramilitary Leaders

On the second night of the prayer walks, amidst growing tension and increased fear, I had arranged to meet with two senior members of the UDA in another part of the Shankill that was opposing C/Company. At first they refused to meet with me; the reason they gave was that they did not want to be told what they should or should not do, but after assurances that this would not be my approach, they agreed to meet. As the meeting began their faces were partially covered and they continued to stand, making it clear I had fifteen minutes and no longer.

I thanked them for their willingness to hear from me, but I made it clear that the meeting was not about me, but about those whose voices remained silent through fear. My appeal was that whatever the main UDA was planning to do against C/Company in the Lower Shankill, they should bear in mind the fact that most people living in that area were innocent and living in fear, and that included rank and file members of C/Company.

They told me, in no uncertain terms, that recent deaths would be avenged, particularly that of the South East Antrim Brigadier whose funeral would be taking place two days after our meeting. It was expected that upwards of 20,000 men would attend. They further told me that immediately following the funeral those same men would invade the Lower Shankill. Their words only served to confirm my worst fears.

I did not try to dissuade them, as I knew it would be pointless. I knew this was what they expected from me, and would have ended the meeting if I tried to do so. My appeal again was for those who were innocent that they would be spared. The fifteen minutes became 50 minutes before the meeting finally came to an end. I later met up with our two prayer walk teams and spent the next three hours walking the streets and praying over a community that had seen more of its share of violence and death, but with the knowledge that it might well see more within the next few days.

The following day I received a call from someone representing the two men I had spoken with the previous evening. I was told that as the meeting was taking place, two cars with armed men were waiting on the meeting to end before entering the Lower Shankill to shoot and kill the first two men they saw, regardless of who they were. However, immediately after the meeting the men in the cars were contacted and were told to call off the attacks. I had further been told that two lives had been spared that night as a direct result of that meeting. So if for no other reason, this made the four week prayer walk worth every step and every prayer, but that was not the end of it, because even more amazing developments were to come.

Our four week prayer walk began on the Monday night. I had the above meeting with the two UDA commanders on the Tuesday night; we were now into Wednesday night, our third night of the prayer walks, but what a night it would be. Things I had been hearing during the day and in the early evening concerned me greatly. It seemed the UDA were not going to wait until after the funeral on Thursday, but were planning something for that Wednesday night. I thought that perhaps an attempt might be made on the life of a prominent member of C/Company within the Lower Shankill.

By the time we met up with the prayer walk teams at 9pm, tensions were at an all-time high. The main UDA within the Shankill sent word to all of their members in C/Company commanding them to defect or to face the consequences. This resulted in several defections to show allegiance to the main UDA, but also resulted in those who remained close and loyal to the rebel Brigadier, now in prison, having to leave their homes for fear of being attacked. Throughout the night, many others were to jump ship, either defecting to the main UDA on the Shankill, or just getting off side by disappearing somewhere, which only served to increase fear in those who remained behind and were still uncertain as to what they should do.

During our prayer walk, I stopped with some of the C/Company members who were still on street duty and encouraged them to be careful during the night. One of them I knew quite well, I said to him: "Listen Sammy. If anyone comes into this street tonight, for goodness sake get off side. You're not going to stop anyone who comes at you with guns." His friend slapped his side and, revealing a gun in his belt, he said, "Let the 'so-and-sos' come. We're ready for them." I told him he was mad and that he and Sammy would be shot. Soon after leaving I went to a home where several men were sitting in darkness, fearful and bewildered.

Midnight was fast approaching. Our prayer walk teams were still on the streets, but were thinking more about home than about anything that might develop during those last moments. Suddenly we heard screaming and shouting. The Lower Shankill was under attack. Up to 200 men in cars and on foot had invaded. Within moments UDA men from other parts of the Shankill had swamped the area. They fought hand to hand with any of the C/Company men who still happened to be in the street; men who were there simply because they were under orders, and not because they wanted to fight.

Like a movie scene

At the time of the attack I immediately made my way to where the fighting was taking place, but within a matter of moments it was over, and there in the darkness I could see cars in the middle of the street as if they had been abandoned; some had their doors open, and others still had their engines running. I also saw several military and police vehicles parked along the street with dozens of heavily armed soldiers and police officers standing alongside their vehicles. As I walked past the military and the police, I could see about twenty men lined up against a gable wall. Each of these men had his back to the wall with his hands raised, in front of each one was a police officer, pointing a gun directly at his head.

The scene looked like a remake of a Lethal Weapon movie, and as I walked through the darkness I heard someone call out: "Hey Pastor Jack! Pastor Jack!" I had no idea who it was, but as I stopped, the person called out again, only this time he shouted: "You came to us for help last night and we did you a favour. Can you do anything to help us?" Puzzled, I looked around, and there standing against the wall was one of the two men I had spoken to for 50 minutes the previous night.

I knew these men were members of a terrorist organisation; I knew they were involved in the feud and had just been involved in an attack on the Lower Shankill. I knew I had often been vocal in my public condemnation of this organisation for various reasons. I knew this same organisation had sentenced me to death on at least one occasion, yet I also knew they had spared two lives the night before, as a result of a meeting I'd had with them, and yet here they were against a wall, under arrest and asking me for help. But what could I do? How could I help them?

So confidently, I approached some of the heavily armed and heavily clad police officers and asked if I could speak with whoever was in charge. I soon found myself straining to look into the eyes of what looked like Darth Vader. There I was, all 5ft 6½in, looking up at an officer who was well over 6ft tall, but who looked much taller, and looked like Darth Vader by the way he was dressed in black protective clothing, his face hidden behind a black face mask and a black protective visor, with a protective helmet on his head.

I remember saying to Darth: "I know those men against the wall are all members of the UDA, but I also know they have effectively dealt with what to them was an internal problem. No one has been killed or seriously injured, and it looks like the feud is over and the arrest of those men will serve no purpose." Leaning over and bending down towards me he asked: "What is it you want me to do?" So I took a deep breath and I whispered: "Let them go!" "What?" he said. Not because he didn't hear me, but because he couldn't believe what I had said! So again I said it, only this time in a louder voice: "Let them go! Just let them go!" He responded by saying: "I can't just let them go. There are other units here from different parts of the city, and there are British soldiers present. I just can't let them go." However, the words were no sooner out of his mouth when another police officer, who had been standing next to him the whole time, listening to our conversation and looking just as invasive, loudly screamed out the words: "Gun, gun!"

That was it. "Gun, Gun!" Immediately he and Darth Vader left me standing alone. They ran for cover behind one of the armoured vehicles, leaving me in the dark, but at the exact same time, in an instant, every police officer and every soldier in the street, including those with guns aimed at the heads of those against the wall, ran for cover behind the armoured Land Rovers. With their backs still against the wall, and their hands still raised in the air, the 20 men turned and looked at each other in total bewilderment and within moments, realising their captors had withdrawn, they ran for their cars that were still sitting in front of them with doors open and engines running.

I could hardly believe what I was seeing. I felt like I had stepped from a scene in Lethal Weapon to a scene in the comedy Police Academy, but this was not an act; and was certainly not a comedy one; this was really happening. The police officers, along with the British soldiers, had taken cover. The men were running to their cars and driving away, and there I was still standing in the centre of the road trying to unravel in my mind what I'd just seen. I didn't hear any gunfire. I saw no guns other than those being carried by the security forces, and I'm thinking: "What just happened there?"

The man who had earlier called out to me and asked for help also jumped into his car, but before driving away he stopped alongside me and said: "Thanks Jack!" And I'm like "What?" He went to say: "You can tell the people in the Lower Shankill it's all over. They've nothing to fear now. They've suffered long enough." And with this he drove off, and all went quiet.

The police and the soldiers came out from behind their vehicles; their prisoners were all gone, but soon they also left, and within moments the streets were even quieter. The immediate result of this was that the Lower Shankill was once again under the control of the main UDA organisation, but with a new Brigadier they had put in place before the dust had even settled, what now for the Shankill?

Even though the feud was effectively over, we continued our prayer walks for the entire four weeks. The feud might well have come to an end on the third night of the prayer walks, but this was not a time to slacken or to drift back inside the church building.

We would continue to stand, walk and pray for the community and for all those affected by this tragic event; an event that brought home the need to fight and win the battle in the heavenly places through prayer and intercession. Knowing that it's this that brings positive results to the troubled streets; something we witnessed first-hand as we not only witnessed the end of the feud, but saw the removal of some of the offensive paramilitary murals on the sides of people's homes. Thanks to a 'friendly' phone call, 18 pipe-bombs mysteriously dropped off on waste ground were discovered by police; some of the older members of the UDA were allowed to leave the organisation; others were sent home after being told they were no longer required to attend weekly meetings or to keep guard at certain homes.

All of the above had taken place within the first three weeks of our prayer walk. The amazing sense of calm was noticeable to all our teams in the Lower Shankill. Compared to what it was like four weeks previously, this was nothing short of miraculous. Yet we remember that men died across Belfast and that families were forever changed by this tragedy, and so we continue to pray for them and for the wider community.

Chapter 22

Healing and Division

Following the Loyalist feuds that caused untold grief, including destruction and death, the community once again showed its resilience by picking up the pieces and by quickly getting back to as normal a life as possible - even though it was known there would still be repercussions, which of course there were. As a church we continued with our prayer walks through the streets, reaching out in our endeavour to bring healing to a hurting community, while at the same time reaching across the divide, as we pursued our dream for reconciliation between our divided communities, which is the core message of the cross.

Even though Northern Ireland has been historically divided by sectarianism along the lines of religion, nationality and culture, the fact remains that within this very division there exist many opportunities for reconciliation, even between those who have been long-standing enemies. As a church we have witnessed people on opposite sides of the conflict, and on either side of the above loyalist feuds, becoming reconciled. Even I, at a personal level, have first-hand experience of such a journey, for I too have known what it is to be reconciled with those who were once my enemies, and I theirs.

Brendan had, for many years, been an active member of the IRA; the organisation that had killed friends and colleagues of mine; the same organisation that had shot family members and had tried to murder me twice. Yet here I was, sitting in our church coffee shop, with this ex-IRA man who had served a life sentence for the murder of a colleague, and yet there we sat drinking coffee and looking into each other's eyes. Looking straight at me he said: "Jack, this is so amazing and can only be God, because there was a time when I would have gladly killed you and when you would have killed me if you'd had the chance, but here we are today, no longer enemies, but brothers in Christ." I responded by saying: "You are so right Brendan, I would have loved to have killed you at one point, but thank God for what he's done in both of our lives." We no longer hated each other.

On another occasion, I met with two other ex-members of the IRA when they attended an event at our church. As we chatted and bantered with each other, one of them said: "Hey Jack! Whenever you were in the UDR, did you believe you were fighting for your country?" I said: "Yes, that was the reason I joined." I was shocked when he said: "We hated the UDR more than we hated anyone!" He continued: "In fact, we hated them more than we hated the paratroopers," and man do I know how much they hated the paras!

As with Brendan, I looked them straight in the eye and said: "Do you know what men? I hated you guys because of what you were doing, and I would have loved at that time to have killed both of you, but God has changed all of that." This was our way of dealing with the past as it affected us, but there was now genuine warmth as we shook hands, not as enemies, but as brothers in Christ, which is something that only God could have done, but not without a price. True reconciliation costs, which is why I am so amazed at the fact that God was willing to pay the price to make reconciliation possible between Him and us, and that the price He paid was nothing less than the death of His only begotten son, as recorded in that amazing verse: *"For God so loved the world that he gave His one and only Son, that whoever believes in Him shall not perish but have eternal life"* (John 3:16).

So when it comes to reconciliation, we as the church should be the first to step up with a willingness to embrace those who are different, without discrimination or regard of colour, creed or even lifestyle, for: *"There is neither Jew nor Gentile, neither slave nor free, nor is there male and female, for you are all one in Christ Jesus."* (Galatians 3:28), but it's easier said than done, for even while some were reaching out and moving forward, others remained hell-bent on flexing muscle and staying in control of communities, which soon became evident in another bloody feud that came much closer to us than we could ever have imagined.

A new depth of despair

This time it was a feud between the UVF and the Loyalist Volunteer Force (LVF) that had been ongoing for several years since the LVF was first formed in 1996; founded by Billy Wright, who was previously a prominent member of the UVF. I had never met him personally, but I did speak with him on the phone. He'd heard that I was facing a death threat from the UVF, so he called to offer his support. He offered to put armed men into our home to remain until the threat was gone. However, I knew this was more of a personal thing between him and the UVF, and had little to do with his desire to protect me, although I do believe that his offer to help was genuine, yet misguided. I also knew that Billy Wright's history was not a pleasant one and that he allegedly had been responsible for up to 20 ruthless murders, although he had never been convicted of any.

So knowing who I was speaking to, I can remember saying to him: "Look Billy, I don't know where you got this from, although I can guess, but while I appreciate your concern and your offer to help, as a Christian and as a pastor I could never accept your offer." He tried to persuade me to reconsider, but I said: "As far I'm concerned Billy, if I need protection I've only got to call the police, but then over and above them, I know God is looking out for me." I heard him laugh, and then he said: "Well look, take down my number and call me if you change your mind." I said: "Billy, I'll not be changing my mind, so I'll not be needing your number." I thanked him again, after which he wished me well and ended the call.

Not long after this Billy Wright was arrested for threatening the life of a woman who was brave enough to report him to the police, and it was while he was in prison on this occasion he was assassinated by members of the Irish National Liberation Army (INLA). However, his death did not unify the feuding factions, but rather, things got worse during the next few years, and especially in 2005 when the feud between them not only came to a head, but came to a violent and bloody end, with the LVF being totally defeated, leaving several of their members dead, even others who were merely 'associated' with the group.

The main stronghold of the LVF was just a few moments' walk from our home. I knew some of its leaders and, for many years, I've been pastor to some of the families within the small community it controlled. One day, as the feud was descending into even lower depths, I heard a frantic knock at our front door. I quickly opened it, and there stood a young lad, just 15 years old. His hood was pulled over his head and was pulled as far down his face as was possible. He looked fearful and frightened, and not waiting too long he quickly said: "Can I come in?" I had no idea who he was, but I knew he needed help, and so I immediately said: "Of course you can come in." Within a moment he was inside sitting down in our living room, but with his hood still over his head. I asked him to remove his hood, and it was only when he did so, I could see he was just a lad.

Having heard his name and having learned where he was from, just a few moments' from our home, I said to him: "So what's been happening?" He said: "They're going to kill me."

"Who's going to kill you?" I asked.

"The UVF" he replied. "They told me I'm dead."

"Wow!" I said. "So why are you here with me?"

He said: "I want you to do my funeral!" It was as much as I could do to hold it together!

I said: "Listen, you're just a kid; there's no one going to kill you! They're just trying to frighten you." I went on to say: "You should be sitting here talking to me about school and about your plans beyond school; you should be talking to me about life, not death." After chatting for a while, and after promising that if anything ever did happen to him, I would conduct his funeral service, but assuring him as best I could do that my services would not be required by him, he allowed me to pray with him before he left.

The UVF continued to make inroads against the LVF, wounding some and killing others. They even shot dead the father of an LVF member as he worked in a shoe shop. It seemed they couldn't get his son, so they shot his 42-year-old father instead. While all this was going on, I had heard nothing more from the young man who came to our home, well not until one night when I was driving through the streets along with two pastors visiting from the USA; one of them a great friend of New Life City Church, Dr Andrew Willis from Houston, Texas, and a mutual pastor friend from Mississippi.

As we drove slowly through the darkened streets, a young man came out of the shadows and approached the car. I stopped and rolled down the window and asked: "What's up?"

He said: "Nothing Pastor Jack! I just knew it was your car." It was the young man who had come to my home.

I asked how he was doing and he said: "I'm doing okay." I introduced him to the pastors in the car and told him to take care. He assured me he would and then walked back into the shadows. He survived the feud while others sadly did not.

An in-flight vision

However, it was during Easter 2005, while the UVF/LVF feud was still raging, I made another visit to the USA. Kathleen, who would normally travel with me, would be joining me one week later, so I was travelling on my own. During the course of the flight something happened that I have only shared a few times, but each time with caution. This is the first time I have put it in writing, but I do so because it is appropriate to what I'm about to share and what was to happen on my return three weeks later. Any time I would cross the Atlantic, I would normally watch a movie and would read at least part of a book, as well as do some work on my laptop, but on that flight, for some reason, I could neither watch a movie nor read a book, but I did pray, which is not something I normally do on the plane, unless I think it's about to crash!

For some reason I had this deep desire to simply seek God, and so I remember putting my face right into my hands and becoming somewhat overwhelmed by a sense of God's presence right there on the plane, and then suddenly, with my face still in my hands, I could see what I can only describe as a vision. Remember Joel said: *"Your old men will dream dreams; your young men will see visions"* (Joel 2:28). In this vision I saw the number 2,000 as it moved across in front of my eyes, appearing from the right and disappearing to the left. It did so three times, but what stood out to me each time, was that the number 2,000 was on fire. Flames were coming out of the top of the entire number. I asked God what this was, and in my mind I could hear His voice. I knew exactly what He said, although I did not fully understand it.

I immediately grabbed a pen and looked for something to write on, but the closest thing to me was a United Airlines paper napkin. So I opened it and began to write the following: 'While sitting on the plane to DC on March 9, 2005. God gave me a vision of the future of New Life City Church. The first thing I saw was a bright tunnel. I was at the broadside – the entrance – looking down through the tunnel encircled with brightness. At the far end I could see a circle of people – there were many. I saw some singing, reading and gathering at what looked like the front of a church hall for ministry and to worship God. I then saw the figure 2,000 flash across from right to left. This happened three times. I could see the figure 2,000 but the figure was burning. God showed me he would take us through the fire to after the fire of His Glory. I still have the paper napkin in my Bible to this day as a reminder of that experience.

The fires begin

The day I returned home to Belfast from the USA, instead of resting for a while, and taking time to get over the jetlag, I was back on the road travelling across the border to Southern Ireland to be involved in an evangelism outreach. I repeated this for the next few days. The last day was March 25. I drove to Dublin and preached in one of the Elim Churches there. The night ended with seven people raising their hands in response to the appeal to commit their lives to Christ. Afterwards I went to the car and switched on my phone and noticed several missed calls from my youngest daughter. She had been trying to contact me for several hours, as my mother, who was in hospital, had been given one hour to live. We were now two hours past the deadline and I was 100 miles away in Dublin.

However, in less than 90 minutes I was in the hospital in Belfast and was standing next to my mother. I had made it on time and was able to speak with her, as she was conscious, but frightened. As the night went on we were told she had settled and that we should go home and rest and come back the next day. Early the following morning I received a phone call from the hospital. Our mother had passed away. I remember the pain of receiving this news. This was my mum who had given much to raise us as best as she could, who, regardless of difficult circumstances, was still able to sing while cooking or doing dishes and could be heard throughout the house as it was a very small home, but she sang so well, and who several years beforehand had committed her life to Christ.

As the pain of this loss took hold of me I remembered the vision on the plane and I cried out to God and said: "Lord, is this the fire?" Then just as surely as I heard the voice on the plane, I heard that same voice say: "No. This is not the fire." Less than two weeks later, and one week after the funeral, I was visited in our home by a well-known UDA commander in North Belfast. He had in his hand a printed copy of an article from Assist News, an American-based Christian News website, where I had made a comment aligning local taxi firms to paramilitary groups, either being owned by them or at least paying protection money to them. He expressed disappointment regarding these comments and stated they were not true, but I made it clear that regardless of his disappointment, I would stand over the comments. He left after midnight, but was obviously far from happy with our conversation. I, however, went to bed feeling quite good, having shown no fear and believing I had actually won him over.

However, a few hours later, around 3.30am, Kathleen and I were asleep, but were suddenly wakened by the sound of breaking glass and by what sounded like an explosion. It rapidly became apparent that our home was being attacked. I immediately jumped out of bed and called out to my son Jonathan. Running downstairs, I foolishly turned off the alarm in case it woke the neighbours. I then opened the door and ran out to the front of the house, but the attackers were already gone. My car was ablaze and the flames were coming dangerously close to our house. Before I could react, a police Land Rover came speeding up the street. It came to an abrupt stop outside our home when two officers jumped out and extinguished the fire within minutes, but it was too late; the car was completely destroyed. The only thing I was able to salvage from the shell was my plastic license that was warped with the heat, but not as warped as those who attacked our home.

I then turned my attention to our home and saw that all of the windows on ground level were completely smashed and covered in paint, except for one which had a Liverpool Football Club logo on it, my favourite football club. So right away I knew Manchester

United fans did not do this! However the point is, these men had the power to do what they wanted, but, Liverpool fans or not, they did not have the right to do so. They had no authority other than the command given to them by someone who had a twisted sense of authority over them. But who was that someone?

While standing in our living room surveying the damage, looking at all the broken glass, seeing pieces of rag that had been attached to the bottles of paint and wondering if they had attempted to light the bottles and burn down the house, and thinking of the night sky being lit up by our car being turned into a fireball, I remembered the vision on the plane and I asked: "Lord, is this the fire?" Again, just like the voice on the plane, I heard: "No. This is not the fire."

The following morning our home was packed with family, friends, church members, some of our pastors, and some very senior politicians. Kathleen and I deeply appreciated the support we received at that time, but were disappointed in the lack of support from the wider church. However, we did receive a visit from someone else that morning. It was the UDA commander who had been in our home the previous night. He offered his condolences, calling those who had carried out this attack 'scum'. He whispered into my ear and asked if I wanted him to retaliate on our behalf. I quickly said: "No way! The police are dealing with it." All this had happened within a few weeks of my experience on the plane, which I'll return to later.

Chapter 23

The Darkness Deepens

Not long after our home had been attacked, and while still carrying out repairs and cleaning up, I received a visit from a senior police officer. He sat in my dining room, on a Friday afternoon, and handed me a sheet of paper, which effectively was a death notice, and he said: "Jack, you need to take this seriously. We have intelligence information that suggests an attempt will be made on your life, and that it could happen during this weekend." He also made it clear that it was not just me, but that others associated with me were in similar danger, although he had no specific intelligence relating to any individual, other than me. I signed his copy of the death notice, and after some security advice from him, he left. It felt quite surreal. I had just been told by a senior police officer who had reliable intelligence that I could be shot that weekend, and I'm left standing with a piece of paper in my hands – ah – but I still had my faith!

The feud between the UVF and the LVF was still in full swing. Joe, who I mentioned earlier in the book, was not only back home from Colorado, but was back in prison. His brother Jameson had been to church several times and had in fact made a profession of faith in Christ, as Joe had done previously. Jameson had his own business and seemed to be doing quite well. He had several younger men working for him, but some of these young men were either in, or were in some way, associated with the LVF. Sadly, this seemed to be enough for the UVF to target him and to accuse him of also being in the LVF, an accusation he totally rejected, and was also rejected by senior leading members of the LVF known to me and with whom I'd met at that time. However, guilt by association is often enough to have someone murdered in Northern Ireland.

While sitting at home one night, my phone rang. It was Jameson. He said: "Jack, the UVF are going to kill me." He made it clear he would not be going anywhere and that if they wanted him, they knew where he lived. Jameson lived in an isolated bungalow just a five minute drive from my home, so I jumped into the car and went and sat with him. We sat for several hours drinking coffee and chatting until after midnight. One of the things he told me was that a few weeks before this, he had paid £40,000 in cash to a UVF commander on the Shankill Road, and for this he was promised protection, but now he was facing a death sentence. I have no way of knowing if this amount of money was ever paid to anyone or how Jameson could possibly have got his hands on this sum, but this was part of his anger as he believed that this payment had secured him protection.

The home was in complete darkness as we watched for a car that we hoped would not appear. I had no idea what we would have done if a car with armed men had pulled up, but believing the night was spent and that no one would be showing up, I finally decided to leave for home, although I knew Jameson would not be going to bed that night. I believed that for that night at least, the danger had passed. We stayed in touch and I met with him several times after this.

A few months passed, and tensions were still running high in our community and in one or two other parts of the city. Summer was approaching and I was personally still raw from the recent attack on our home. On those grounds, I made the decision to express my disgust about the UVF. I purposely chose July 1 as this is a special day for the UVF every year, and I did so because I believed the UVF had been involved in intimidating me and other members of our church whose taxis had been firebombed, and who I also believed had been involved in the late night attack on our home. However, I was later told the attack had been carried out as a joint venture with the UDA commander who had sat in my home the night before the attack occurred.

On July 1 every year, the memories of thousands of brave soldiers from across the UK and Ireland, who had sacrificed their lives for freedom in Europe during World War 1, are honoured. The main commemorations in Belfast are for those men of the 36th Ulster Division who died during the Battle of the Somme, near the Somme River in France. Some of these commemorations are held by the UVF in Belfast, an organisation that traces its roots back to the formation of the Ulster Volunteers in 1912 that became the UVF in 1913; initially formed to fight against the IRA in Ireland, but when war broke out in Europe, many within the UVF joined the newly formed 36th Ulster Division. Two years later, the men of the 36th Ulster Division were going 'over the top' at the Battle of the Somme on July 1, 1916, which resulted in around 8,500 of their men being either killed or seriously wounded. They fought and died honourably. 'From the rising of the sun, until the going down of the same, we will remember them.'

Memorial Day desecrated by murder

So it was on this anniversary of the Battle of the Somme, July 1, 2005, that I chose to walk along the middle of the Shankill Road while carrying the cross with John 3:16 inscribed on it. I did so because those men of the 36th Ulster Division who died at the Somme died for freedom, not for tyranny. In fact they died fighting against the tyrants in Europe at that time. Yet while there is much to honour the memory and the sacrifice of those men, the actions of some are a disgrace to their memory.

I was accompanied by several members of our church, but

also by a number of Christians from a church in Virginia. They walked along the pavement giving away 1,000 copies of my second book, The Cross and the Gun to pedestrians and motorists. I wore a white t-shirt with the words; The Cross is mightier than the Gun, on the back.

However, shortly before I began the walk, someone leaned into my ear and said: "Pastor, Jameson has just been shot dead!" I was shocked, saddened, and angered. His £40,000 did not save him! His assassins picked a moment when he was totally off guard and was at his most vulnerable. At around 10am in broad daylight, 25-year-old Jameson was shot several times as he sat in his truck, but not before, though wounded, screaming out to his young helper and telling him to run.

Fighting back the emotion I felt at that time, I picked up the cross and began to walk, but with a new sense of determination and outrage. Yes of course, the cross represents the fact that Jesus died for all and of forgiveness that is available to all who embrace it, but there is another side to the cross that is represented by the two who died on either side of Jesus, where one embraced forgiveness, while the other spurned and rejected it. So as I walked with the cross that day, I felt I was not simply promoting forgiveness, but was declaring the reality of judgment on all who rejected its message.

As I walked along the centre of the Shankill Road, I approached the headquarters of the UVF that has its offices right there on the front of the street. The news of Jameson's death was still very raw, as was my anger. So when I got to the UVF offices I instinctively made an impromptu stop in the middle of the road where I stood with my back to the offices for five minutes as a point of protest at Jameson's death, and in the hope they would at least read the back of the t-shirt The Cross is mightier than the Gun.

My thoughts turned towards Joe, who was in prison at the time of the murder. Less than a year previously they had buried their young sister Denise, only 17-years-old, who sadly died as the result of a rare heart disorder caused by drugs that, according to rumours at the time, were supplied by members of the UDA, and now Joe was about to hear of the death of his young brother Jameson. I soon visited Joe in prison and was amazed at how calm he was; yes he was angry, and yes he was broken-hearted, but there was a sense of calmness about him that I had not seen before. Jameson's funeral was officiated by one of my associate pastors at that time, Mark Armstrong, along with my son Jonathan who was our then youth pastor. Unfortunately Joe was unable to attend due to death threats, but he took comfort in the knowledge that Jameson had committed his life to Christ.

The feud finally came to an end in 2006 with the demise of the LVF that was effectively put out of business by the much larger and much stronger UVF.

Chapter 24

A New Door Opens

Bible College did not have classes on how to deal with paramilitary feuds, or death threats and attacks on your home. I suppose the expectation was that you just got on with conducting church services and growing the church as best you could, and if they didn't hear from you again until you retire, well that would be fine. So I suppose I should have learned, after all that Kathleen and I had come through, that it was now time to settle back for the next 10 years and arrive safely at retirement age – or was it?

2005 was a very painful year. It was the year I lost my mother; the year our home was attacked; the year I signed for the receipt of a death notice; and the year another young man connected to New Life City Church was shot and murdered. However, before the end of the year, someone told me that a large warehouse was for sale in a street that links the Protestant Shankill with the Catholic Falls Road. My first thought was: 'Why do people tell me these things?' I drove past to see what the building was like and I immediately knew this was for us, but the moment we submitted an offer, someone came in with a better one. Our first bid was £800,000 but within a few weeks we were bidding close to £1million.

One day my phone rang. It was someone from the Shankill

Road. He said: "Jack, I hear you're trying to buy the James E Ball warehouse."

I said: "Yep, we are." He then said: "If you meet me tomorrow night at 10.30pm in a car park at Mallusk with £50,000 cash in a bag, we'll make sure you get the building!" I said: "Are you kidding? I'm not meeting anyone at 10.30pm at night with £50,000 cash in a bag." He was getting nowhere, so the call ended. Two weeks later the estate agent called me and said: "I've heard through the grapevine that the building has been sold from under our noses." He was more concerned that he was losing out on the commission, but it seemed someone was not. So the building was sold.

Everyone at New Life was really disappointed, we now wanted a warehouse, and it seemed like almost any warehouse would do. So we searched around Belfast for seven months looking for a warehouse, and all the time we were looking, some of our ladies were going round to this one in Northumberland Street and praying over it. They even anointed the railings with oil. They would often tell me what they were doing and would say, "Pastor, that building is ours!" For seven months they did this, and for seven months I would say: "Listen ladies, the building is sold!" At one point I remember saying: "Read my lips ladies, the building is sold." But they continued to do what they did, while we, the spiritual leadership, continued looking for a warehouse in another part of the city - in fact we almost clinched a deal with another building, but the estate agent called, seven months later, and he said: "Are you still interested in buying the warehouse in Northumberland Street?"

I said: "Why are you asking?"

He said: "Because it's back on the market; the other deal has fallen through!" I can tell you that this pastor had to go and eat a lot of humble pie and apologise to those ladies who had prayed faithfully for those seven months. We made an offer of £1.1million that was accepted and the building was ours.

While the purchase of the building was miraculous, we were broke, so we spent the next three years trying to raise enough to refurbish it. Due to the location of the building, which I'll explain further in a moment, and due to the nature of our work that is both spiritual and social in terms of our community outreach programmes, we believed we would receive support from major funding sources and from Christian businessmen. In spite of many hours of effort and meetings, and yes, much prayer, we were unsuccessful in securing any funds to refurbish. We had no other option, but to secure a loan from the bank to at least do enough work so we could move into the building and begin to conduct services and create a daily presence in that location through our community outreach programmes.

Inside the building today we have an auditorium which comfortably seats 600, although we have had worship concerts with up to 1,300 standing. It is mainly used for church services, concerts, worship events and conferences. We also have a pre-school playgroup with 24 children attending each morning, an after-school club for children with additional needs, parents and toddlers and parent support groups, outreach programmes for men, women and young people, and in-depth personal development programmes for all ages, from youths to adults. We have a coffee shop which is open daily and most nights to the public. We also have an indoor 3G-soccer pitch that caters for teams with five or six players on each side, and which was funded, a few years after we had moved in, by Sport NI (a Northern Ireland government department), and which has been an amazing addition to our services.

What is unique and exciting about the building is not just what happens inside, but it's the location. The building literally straddles the main dividing line between Protestants and Catholics within our area of Belfast. Half the building is on one side of the divide and half the building is on the other side. This means we are literally working in both communities, by not only reaching out to where they were, because we are part of them, but by drawing people together inside the building. We have staff, volunteers and many users from both sides, even those who have been actively involved in the conflict as combatants.

This is our miracle

It has taken us several years of trusting God and of doing what we were able to do, to get where we are today, but we are here due to the faithfulness of God and the faithfulness of volunteers. We deeply appreciate that although we received no funding to help with the refurbishment of the building, we have been successful at securing support for some of our programmes and overheads, and for some salaries from government and other funding sources. However, I've often said: 'Our miracle is, that we are where we are today, not because someone stepped up and handed us a cheque for a million pounds, but we are where we are today in spite of the fact that no one ever did hand us a cheque for a million pounds. Although we of course remain open to that possibility!

There was a moment, however, when we almost gave up. I had been serving on our movement's executive leadership team in Ireland with the responsibility for evangelism throughout the island of Ireland. My focus was not to open a church in any location just for the sake of having a church there, but to strengthen and help develop those churches which were struggling, but still had a desire and a sense of calling to their community. Give me a man with a sense of calling and with vision for a community, and let me help that man fulfil that vision, rather than a location to simply plant a church and then try to find someone who will go and lead that work for a few years before moving on somewhere else.

While trying to find the time to not only give leadership and direction to our movement's evangelism, but to also provide leadership at other levels, I was struggling to balance this with the development of New Life City Church and with the move to our new building. At one point things got so tight financially that I had a personal and serious heart to heart talk with our then Irish Superintendent, Pastor Eric McCombe, who, along with his wife Ruth, gave great support to Kathleen and me and to the work we were doing at New Life. During our conversation, Eric suggested I hand back the keys of the building. He said: 'Jackie, give me back the keys, and take New Life to another Elim Church and take things forward there.'

From a financial perspective that would have been so easy to do, but not when I knew I was pursuing vision and the call of God right where I was; so I respectfully declined the offer, after which I resigned from Elim's Irish leadership team for the purpose of committing myself wholeheartedly to the development of New Life City Church and its community outreach programmes. The intervening years have shown that was the right decision.

We formally moved in at the end of October 2009, but not without some amazing God-moments. For 40 days prior to the official opening, I had decided to do a 40-day cross vigil, that is standing with the cross with JOHN 3:16 on it right next to our new building, but between the main dividing gates that to this day are shut at nights thereby creating a small piece of no-man's land between the two communities. It was there I stood for 40 days between the gates and the communities for three hours each day. I was supported by Colin Morrison, who was with us at New Life City Church for almost two years before returning to New Zealand where he and his wife Carol pioneered and pastored the Elim church in Invercargill.

Motorists beeped their horns at us and cheered us on. Many came and stood with us to speak and to encourage us, to pray and to be prayed for, and they did so from both sides of the divide. However, although there were many amazing things that happened, one day stands out. It was during the third week. Colin had just left and I was putting the cross into my car when a motorcyclist pulled up beside me. At first I was a bit disconcerted. I had no idea who he was and why he was there. He removed his helmet and he said:

"Pastor Jack, can I speak with you for a moment?" Feeling a bit more confident now that his helmet was off and I could see his face, I was happy to hear what he had to say.

He told me he had ridden past several times looking for an opportunity to stop and chat, but there was always someone standing speaking with me, so he just rode on past.

He said: "I knew you finished at this time of the day and I thought it would be the best time to catch you for a few moments." Somewhat nervously he continued to tell me he was not long out of prison, where he'd been for two years. He then said: "Hardly a day went by that I never thought of coming to speak with you and to ask for your forgiveness."

I said: "What is it I need to forgive you for?"

He said: "Well the night your home was attacked, I was the one who led the attack. It's not something I wanted to do, but I was under orders."

He never told me who had given the order to carry out the attack, and I never went there, as I knew he was taking a chance even speaking with me. After chatting for a few moments, I said to him: "Look, you need to know that the night you attacked our home was the night my wife and I forgave you."

I then said: "But hey, if you need to know you're forgiven, then I'm telling you now, I forgive you." We shook hands as I told him there were no hard feelings, and then parted company, but not before I invited him to church, although I've not seen him since.

Within a few weeks our new facility called City Life Centre was officially opened. Our own worship team led us in a great time of celebration, but we also had a special guest choir for the evening, the Omagh Waterford Peace Choir. We had an amazing night and have continued since to grow and develop our outreach.

We are becoming more multi-cultural, with people from

various parts of Africa, Europe, the USA and the Philippines joining with us regularly and becoming actively involved in the life and ministry of the church, along with several from both communities in Belfast and many others who travel from outside Belfast to be with us each week and to support our outreach.

City Life Centre and *New Life City Church* has become light in a dark place. Many find help by simply dropping in, or by joining some of our support and personal development programmes, or by attending church or some of our special outreach programmes. We thank God for those who have come to personal faith in Christ while sitting in this converted warehouse, whether in a church service or by just meeting with someone in our coffee shop.

One Sunday morning I was delighted that Joe, Jameson's brother mentioned earlier, brought a friend and neighbour to church with him. The young man is the son of one of the two brothers who had tried to kill me, mentioned in Chapter Five. I was further delighted that at the end of the message he raised his hand to indicate his desire to commit his life to following Jesus Christ. He is one among many from various backgrounds who have made that same decision sitting in a converted warehouse that straddles the dividing wall and the dividing gates in Belfast. *"You will call your walls Salvation and your gates Praise"* (Isaiah 60:18).

Chapter 25

Ireland – Not Just An Island

By the year 2011, we were still settling into our new facility, but even though we had faced some early difficulties, we were growing as a church and as an outreach to the wider community. However, the significance of that year cannot be overstated. I say this for two reasons: It was the year we brought Arthur Blessett back to Belfast, which I will refer to in more detail in the next chapter, and was also the year I preached a message entitled, 'Ireland is not just an Island, it's His land.'

"Listen to me, you islands; hear this, you distant nations: Before I was born the LORD called me; from my mother's womb he has spoken my name" (Isaiah 49:1).

Note that in the above verse a call goes out to the islands and to the distant nations, showing that God does not only have a word for Israel, but that He also has a word for the islands and for the nations, and just in case you might have missed it, let me remind you that Ireland is an island, often referred to as the Emerald Isle. However, there's something special about this island, and it's not just in the name, but is in the fact that Ireland is not just an island; it is His Land.

The fact that God specifically mentions 'islands' means it is safe to assume that islands are God's little gifts of earth that are sprinkled across the oceans, like precious jewels for our enjoyment. Ireland is one of those islands that God has gifted to the world, with tens of millions of its sons and daughters who have made significant contributions to the development of other nations across the world, not least America.

It was around 1997, during one of my visits to the USA, while attending an American/Ireland investment conference at the White House organised by President Bill Clinton, that the President said: "America owes much to the three big "I's" - the Israelis, the Italians and the Irish." Now I can only suggest what the Israelis and the Italians might have contributed to American society and to its history, but I can comment with some authority on what Ireland has contributed.

Besides providing the USA with thousands of soldiers who fought and died in the War Of Independence and who later fought on both sides of the American Civil War, our little island has also given individuals like Neil Armstrong – the first man to walk on the moon; Davy Crockett, who fought and died at the Alamo; Bono and U2, Liam Neeson, and Pierce Brosnon, as well as 17 American presidents to date, whose ancestral roots are in Ireland, besides many of the existing officers in the NYPD and NYFD, and so it goes on.

So given that Ireland is one of God's little gifts to the world, it is not surprising that Ireland is not only an island filled with hatred, but is an island that is hated so vehemently by the devil himself. Like Israel, we are loved by God, but hated by the devil, which is why Ireland has been plagued with internal conflict for centuries, and even in recent history has been stained with the blood of many of its sons and daughters; blood that was shed not by invaders or by strangers in our midst, but shed by the hands of fellow Irishmen and women. Patrick might well have lifted the message of the cross throughout this island, but emissaries of satan, ancient and modern, have lifted the sword, the spear and the gun, and have become the perpetuators of a blood curse upon Ireland.

The Hound of Ulster

The Legend of an ancient Irish Warrior, Cu Chulainn (pronounced Ko Hoolin), places him in the first century of Irish history, around the time of Christ. His birth name was Setanta, but was changed to Cu Chulainn when he slew a fierce guard dog with a hurling stick and ball, smashing the ball into the throat of the dog and killing it. The dog belonged to a blacksmith called Culain, who was a friend of Setanta's uncle and foster father, King Conor of Ulster. On seeing how distraught Culain had become at the loss of his prized guard dog, Setanta vowed to take the place of the fallen dog to defend and protect Ulster, the northernmost province in Ireland, most of which makes up Northern Ireland today.

From that day onward, Setanta became known as Cu Chulainn, the Hound of Culain, but more often referred to as *The Hound of Ulster*. He became a man feared by many, killing even his best friend and his equal in a one to one combat that lasted for several days, but also killed his own son in tragic circumstances. He predicted his own fame, and declared that his accomplishments would be spoken of among the stories of the great heroes of his people, declaring: "I care not whether I die tomorrow or next year, if only my deeds live after me," which of course they have.

I once heard it said that Cu Chulainn stood on a rock that today overlooks Belfast, and lifting his spear over Ulster, a spear that had shed the blood of many, he declared that blood would not cease to flow throughout Ireland. For this reason, some would say he placed a 'blood curse' upon the land that remains to this day. I am not certain how true this part of the story actually is, but what I do know is that Cu Chulainn was gripped and driven by a personal blood curse upon his own life that caused him to kill relentlessly, and to likewise die a bloody death on the battlefield with his trusted spear in hand.

Even today across the island of Ireland, Cu Chulainn is hailed as a hero, but ironically, just like St Patrick, both Protestants and Catholics claim Cu Chulainn as their respective ancient hero. Nationalists, mainly within the Catholic community, would regard him as an Irish hero, while unionists, mainly within the Protestant community, would portray him as an Ulster hero, because he serves as a symbol of an undefeated cause and an undefeated people. Sadly, the curse of Cu Chulainn is still being fulfilled throughout Ireland to this day, but especially in Ulster. It's because Ireland has a special place in the purposes of God - it is hated by the hater of creation, the devil himself.

Our response

So what should our response be? Well first of all, for those of us who live here and are Christians, we need to stay focused on the fact that we are here for a purpose. We were not born into another generation, nor were we born in another place - we were born here, in this place, at this time, and for such a time as this. As the church, we are the presence of Christ on earth so that wherever we are, God has a word for us, and he says: "Listen to me you islands, whether large or small; listen to me. Ireland, listen to me, you distant nations; America, listen to me," but the problem is, we're not listening.

God has a word for us today, but many are not listening. He has a word for Ireland. He has a word for America. He has a word for Israel. He has a word for the islands and for the nations, and that word is to be communicated through us, the church. But before He can get the word through the church, He has to get the word to the church; not through the Northern Ireland Assembly in Belfast; not through the Knesset in Tel Aviv, and not through the White House in Washington DC, but through the church. Let's not be too eager to hear what the politicians are about to say, but let's allow the politicians to wonder what we, the church, are about say, but then let's say what we say, because we have heard from God.

So what is God saying? Well this I believe is what God has

said to me. He's saying He is going to restore the destiny of Ireland, both north and south. An island, His land, of two peoples, two nations, and two cultures, but who all by birth-right belong to this emerald isle. It's an island that has lost its way, because it has been lured from its original destiny that was to be a launching pad for the Gospel of Christ to the nations of the world. God is restoring a fresh sense of destiny so that Ireland will once again touch the nations with the message of the cross.

God is also saying that He is restoring Ireland to its former glory; an island that once was ablaze with the glory of God, but one that for centuries has been covered in darkness. God will not restore the destiny of this island without also restoring its former glory, regardless of its bloody violent past. Once again the fires of worship that burned for centuries will burn again with such heartfelt Spirit anointed worship, so that Ireland will again be FIRELAND, revealing the glory of God to the nations.

Within just a few days of preaching this message (the above and more) I received a phone call from a pastor friend and colleague, Brian Madden. He told me that Roy Fields, a well-known worship leader who has been used by God across the USA, Africa and Europe, and also the UK, was coming to Ireland in April 2012. He wanted to come to Northern Ireland, but specifically to Belfast to lead special revival services each Friday to Sunday over four weekends. At that moment I thought – my next visit to the USA is April 2012 and I'm already booked to speak in several churches, but I cannot let this pass, and I cannot miss what God has planned to do among us. I immediately agreed that Roy Fields could come and spend those weekends with us at New Life City Church, and for the first time since 1985 I cancelled my visit to the USA, and was blessed by God for having done so.

Those weekends are among some of the most memorable times at New Life City Church, especially since having moved to our new building at the dividing line, for during those weekends it was again confirmed that our *"walls would be called Salvation and our gates Praise.*" (Isaiah 60:18). The worship would last for at least two hours each night, with Roy also speaking and ministering into people's lives for another two hours. People came from near and far. Lives were changed as people were saved, healed, restored and encouraged in their faith, but those weekends also laid down another significant milestone in the ongoing journey of New Life City Church.

This was also the start of a great relationship with Roy and with his wife Melanie and their family, both here in Ireland and in the USA. Each time Roy has come back to Belfast, since his first visit, he has brought Melanie, when she would join with him in ministry and would often preach, and man does she pack a punch when she preaches! Together they have greatly impacted both our lives as well as many others within New Life City Church. We've always believed in the significance of worship, but Roy and Melanie's times with us helped us to another level and to further depths.

Their visits were also part of the journey that led to the launch of FIRELAND, a worship event that we hold on the last Sunday night of each month when together, along with others who join us, we enter an extended time of worship, pouring out our hearts before God, seeking His face and being open to receive whatever He has prepared for us as a church and as individuals. At FIRELAND we believe a fire can be lit across Ireland with worship and the word. Perhaps God will use us to light that fire. This should be the desire of every church fellowship, regardless of size or standing, and the longing of every believer, that whatever God is going to do He can do it through me, just like Baptist pastor, J. Edwin Orr wrote in 1936 while preaching in New Zealand:

O Holy Ghost, revival comes from Thee
Send a revival, start the work in me
Thy Word declares, Thou wilt supply our need
For blessings now, O Lord, I humbly plead.

Chapter 26

Lifting the Cross Higher and Further

Having walked with the cross for 40 days in 2002, I never thought I would carry it again, yet I did for one day in 2005 a few months after our home had been attacked and the day Jameson was shot dead, but for me that was it! However, God had other ideas, because in 2009, when we were moving into our new building, I felt compelled by God to stand with the cross for 40 days in an area between the dividing gates we call *no man's land*. Having done it again I thought that was finally it; the cross was being put away for good, but then again, God had other plans.

CU@ theCROSS

Many young people in Belfast fall victim to suicide. For many this is a serious option as a way of escape from their circumstances. The entire community feels the impact of every suicide and of every family, which has been devastated by the tragic loss of a loved one. Normally the only time the church is involved is when it's too late, when the life has been taken and the family has been thrown into grief. Churches on hearing of such loss would pray for those families, and church ministers would call and offer condolences and prayers and would later officiate at the funeral service.

I do not highlight the above as a point of criticism against the church, but as a simple statement of fact. This is how it is, but churches would love it to be different and would love to be able to do more to help, as would so many organisations across the community. It was in response to several suicides across our community, some known to me personally, that this feeling of wanting to do more caused me to call out to local churches, challenging them to come together to reach out to the community, and especially to those who were hurting; to come together in a visible and tangible way, and with a message of hope and an offer to help. Many responded from within Belfast and beyond, and also from Dublin, from England, and from various denominations, which led to an event called CU@ theCROSS.

Our objective was to send a clear message that there was better way than suicide and that help was available within the community. We did so recognising the good work carried out by legitimate community groups, but also showing that help was available within the church. We erected a 20ft cross between the dividing gates right next to the church. This 20ft cross, clearly visible on both sides of the gates, became our gathering point for CU@ theCROSS.

The plan was for four groups of marchers to make their way to the cross between the gates. These groups would come from north, south, east and west Belfast, with each group being led by someone carrying a cross, so we had four processions across Belfast. Some of those churches that took the lead or became the starting point for each walk were, the Elim Christian Centre, Karmel City Church, Kingsway Fellowship Church, Maghaberry Elim, and Ballygomartin Presbyterian, who were supported by several other churches. Several church leaders not only led from the front, but also participated at various stop-off points along the way for prayers and Bible readings. John Edwards, from Walking Free Ministries in England, joined us with his cross. Duncan Hanson and his wife from South Africa who are now ministering in England also joined us, as did the Give Way to Jesus Team in Northern Ireland, who also supplied us with three large crosses for the day.

However, while it was great to see churches and church leaders coming together in this way, I felt the jigsaw was incomplete; something was missing. It was then I began to think of the possibility of inviting Arthur Blessitt to join with us as our special guest for CU@ theCROSS. Arthur had an outreach on Sunset Boulevard in Los Angeles during the late 1960s and 70s, but he became famous by carrying a cross literally around the world for almost 50 years. The first time he ever walked with the cross outside of the USA was in 1971 when he came to Northern Ireland. I was a young Christian at that time, and I was mesmerized by the sight of this man walking by with a cross over his shoulder, just a few feet from where I was standing alone. And now, 40 years later, I am planning an event called CU@ theCROSS, in that very same street, and right beside that very spot where Arthur Blessitt passed me in 1971.

I did not know Arthur Blessitt personally, and he certainly did not know me, or anything about me. I found out he lived in Denver, Colorado, obtained his phone number and gave him a call. Within moments I was speaking one to one with Arthur Blessitt, and to my great delight he immediately accepted my invitation to join with us for CU@ theCROSS in June 2011. It turned out to be an amazing event with several hundred coming together and with several thousand seeing the cross lifted and carried across Belfast. While others joined with us, I counted it a personal honour at one point to walk alongside Arthur Blessitt with both of us carrying a cross along the very street where I had first seen him exactly 40 years earlier. Now that just had to be the work of God.

Worth every step

The event did not end the blight of suicide within Northern Ireland, but it did lift the cross throughout the city of Belfast, and it did bring many believers and fellowships together, and it did at least save one life that we know of. While walking with crosses we handed out thousands of leaflets, one of which showed there is a better way than suicide. One of our marchers put this leaflet through a letterbox in a door, not knowing that at that precise moment a young man was standing on a chair and was about to end his life. He heard the noise at the door and stepped off the chair to see what it was, and there on the floor was a little tract showing there is a better way than suicide. It caused him to open the door and to connect with some of the marchers who prayed with him and led him to faith in Christ. If only for him, the event was worth every step.

The 20ft cross was erected only for that one event and was to be taken down soon afterwards. However, it remained in place for over three years. During those years the cross stood high above the dividing gates and could be clearly seen from both sides of the divide. It fact, it was even used by some on Sundays as a point of access to the church, because on Sundays the gates were closed, which meant that anyone coming to church from the Catholic side of the gates had to drive or walk to other access points in the dividing wall, but some chose instead to climb the gates and slide down the cross to get into church.

However, after three years of enduring the elements, the cross finally came down by itself, but by then we no longer needed it for access purposes as we had managed by the end of 2011 to secure the opening of the dividing gates on Sundays by negotiation with the Department of Justice and with the Community Relations Commission. We do, however, miss seeing the cross that stood high above the gates, but perhaps someday we will replace it with a more permanent one. So was that it then? Was that the end of the *cross walks?* Well I personally had no other plans, but within a year I was to discover, as at other times, that God did!

During this same period we took a further leap beyond our comfort zone when we launched a new outreach on the Catholic side of the dividing wall called Falls Community Fellowship. The Falls outreach is led by Tony Meehan who came onto our pastoral team with the responsibility of developing this ministry. Several doors have opened to us, not least a club belonging to the political wing of the official IRA who let us have an upstairs room free of charge for a Sunday night service. While we sang and worshipped and shared testimonies etc, several would come in from the bar, drinks in hand, and would hang around and listen to what was being shared. This story is still unfolding and other doors are opening to enable us to reach further and deeper into the community both spiritually with prayer and services, and practically by providing tons of food weekly from our food bank to families caught in the poverty trap.

To help promote our outreach to the city of Belfast and beyond, and to help raise support for our work, we decided to take our message to America in a unique and demanding way.

Cycle Cross America

It was in 2012 when, after discussions with a few of our church members and friends, we decided to take the cross with JOHN 3:16 to the USA. The venture was called Cycle Cross America, and involved four cyclists. Our cyclists were John Cartmill, the team leader, and Les Clarke, both from the Protestant side of the wall, with Kevin McIlkerney and Andrew Higgins from the Catholic side of the wall, who together had spent months preparing physically and psychologically for this challenge, cycling from Los Angeles, California, to Jacksonville, Florida. I went along as the leader and main organiser, making contacts with churches across America for support, sleeping accommodation, parking and preaching opportunities, besides helping to drive the RV support van, but also carrying the cross through cities in every state along the way. We were also joined by Charlie Farrell, an excellent friend from Toms River, New Jersey, who became our main driver and cook. He also walked in front of the cross playing the bagpipes, dressed in a kilt and beret.

Cycle Cross America began on September 22 at Santa Monica Beach where the cyclists dipped the back wheels of their bikes into the Pacific Ocean. Afterwards we made our way to Sunset Boulevard where I carried the cross for several miles, led by Charlie playing the bagpipes and flanked by our four cyclists. We walked past the building that at one time was called *His Place*, the ministry led by Arthur Blessitt before he came to Belfast in 1971. We were very well received along Sunset Boulevard and also when we finally reached Hollywood Boulevard. Afterwards the cyclists made their way back to the Dream Centre where we had been staying for a few nights beforehand.

The following day we were welcomed by Pastor Matthew Barnet to Angelus Temple where we had the opportunity of sharing for 15 minutes during the morning service. After the service the cyclists began their journey which would take them across America. They arrived safely in Jacksonville on October 24. We concluded with a walk to the White House with me carrying the cross, led by Charlie and his bagpipes, and flanked by the four cyclists. That evening we were invited to a reception, facilitated and hosted by the Director of the Northern Ireland Bureau in Washington DC, with special guests, food, drinks, and music by Charlie's band, Clan Suibhne (Sweeny); a welcome and a fitting end to our five weeks on the road.

There are many amazing stories of hospitality, open and closed doors, dangers, tumbles, rattle snakes, scorpions, road runners, ministry opportunities and new friendships that have lasted to this day, including almost being arrested twice. One of those occasions was in Las Cruces, New Mexico. It was so ironic that a pastor from Northern Ireland was threatened with the possibility of arrest in Las Cruces, the *City of the Crosses* for carrying a cross, but thankfully the arrest was avoided. The other occasion was in San Antonio where we walked through several streets to the Alamo and where I was threatened with arrest by a police officer if I brought the cross onto the sidewalk around the Alamo. I felt the spirit of Davy Crockett (an American-Irish fighter at the Alamo) coming upon me, but I resisted. The police officer permitted me to stand on the road with my heel firmly fixed against the curb of the pavement, but not on it. So we stood there for an hour or more without being arrested.

Anyway, regardless of all the mishaps, we made it all the way across from the Pacific Ocean where the back wheels of the bikes had been dipped, to the Atlantic Ocean where the front wheels were dipped. This was followed by a welcome swim in the ocean, before making our way to Washington DC. We deeply appreciate all those who helped us along the way, from Los Angeles to Jacksonville and beyond. A special mention must go to Marcie Gronenthal, her father Ray and daughter Katie in Los Angeles and our mutual friend Jenny Pillo who went out of their way to do so much to make sure we had a great start to Cycle Cross America. They were there for us. Five weeks on the road and it was time for home, and was also time to hang up the cross once and for all – well so I thought!

Thirty-nine plus one (39+1)

In 2013 I was back at Church on the Rock in Alaska for the second time, but this time it was to speak at their annual missions' conference. At one of the gatherings, a young woman from Honduras talked about an outreach called *One Nation One Day*. Throughout the conference I found myself making reference to this young woman who was bold enough to believe that her nation could be saved or changed in a day, and made the point several times that God is looking for those who are just as bold to believe their nation can be saved or changed in a day.

While sitting around a dinner table with some of the pastors, we were discussing how things had been going at the conference. I found myself again making reference to the belief that a nation could be saved or changed in a day, and at that moment it was like déjà vu! It seemed like I'd previously experienced this, when once again I believe the Holy Spirit planted the seed of an idea deep into my spirit; a seed that consisted of nothing more than two numbers, 39+1. During the next few weeks that same seed grew into a vision that was finally brought to fruition in 2014 with a Belfast citywide outreach called 39+1.

The 39 represented 39 days of spiritual and practical renewal with activities to facilitate and encourage change in hearts and lives across Belfast and beyond. The 39 days culminated on one special day, which was Good Friday, April 2014. During the 39 days we encouraged change in individuals, change in the church, change in the community, change in the city and change in the nation. We challenged drug dealers to cease selling drugs during those days, not naïve enough to believe they would, but bold enough to at least challenge them to do so. We did the same with paramilitary groups, and we challenged political groups and other organisations caught up in confrontational situations in Belfast to find a way forward.

During the actual 39+1 days many from New Life City Church stepped up to the mark, joined and supported by several from other churches. We were blessed to see our people from both sides of the dividing wall joining together in *cross walks* and static cross vigils. One of the most amazing days was when one of our women from the Falls, Fiona, carried the cross along the Falls Road. She then handed it to Tommy, an ex-UVF Commander, as she passed through the dividing gates and he then carried it along the Shankill Road. As well as the *cross walks* and static cross vigils located at conflict and major interface areas across the city, we also erected a prayer tent between the dividing gates where many from both sides stopped for prayer and where some committed their lives to Christ.

The entire event culminated with the unveiling of a new cross, the *Cross of Crosses*, between the dividing gates, and with 39+1 hours of non-stop worship from the evening of Good Friday until noon on Easter Sunday. This was attended by many throughout the 40 hours and led by singers, worship leaders and worship teams from various churches.

There are many amazing stories of positive and confrontational meetings, of opportunities to talk with people, pray for people, and to lead some to faith in Christ, and of opportunities to meet with some very significant community and political leaders in the hope of influencing the decision makers in our city. However, 39+1 was not without its tragedies.

Chapter 27

The Man with the White Guitar

We were five days into a 40 Day cross vigil, standing between embittered rivals in the northern part of Belfast, lifting the cross, not only as a symbol of God's love, but a symbol of reconciliation. We stood between Protestants to our left and Catholics to our right. It was the afternoon of March 14. Two men shouted to us from the Catholic side of the road, which was not unusual as people would often shout at us, but this was different. One of the two men was more vocal than the other, and was carrying a white guitar. At first, due to the noise of the traffic, we could not make out what he was shouting, but he didn't give up. On the third attempt I could clearly hear the man with the white guitar shout out: "What's that? John 3:16?"

I shouted back: "Do you want me to come over and explain it to you?"

He shouted: "Yes, come on," and waving his hand he beckoned me over. So I left the relative safety of our little spot between the communities, and crossed over to the Catholic side of the road.

To break the ice I immediately asked him: "Can you play that guitar?"

He said: "Yes," and without asking, he voluntarily got down on one knee, put the guitar over his lap and started to strum and sing.

After a few brief moments he laughed and stood to his feet, but as he stood up he asked me: "What's that you're doing over there?" This gave me the opportunity to share with him and his friend the reason we were standing with the cross, and the opportunity to explain John 3:16. Both he and his friend expressed concern for our safety, because they knew, as did we, that we were standing between both communities in quite a volatile situation.

I gave each of them a Max Lucado tract that had 'John 3:16' on the front and had a good explanation of the verse on the inside. I took them through the tract and through John 3:16. At the end of our chat the man with the white guitar reached out his hand and as he shook my hand he said: "Fair play to ya." He then pointed back to the spot where we were standing and said: "You be careful over there. That's dangerous ground."

I said: "I know mate, but there's someone much bigger who is looking out for us." He smiled and off he went with his friend, both with a Max Lucado tract in their hands.

It was such a great story that I told it several times over the weekend, describing the men as being in their thirties and describing the one with the white guitar as having a nose that looked like someone had smashed him in the face with a hammer and had broken it. But, little did I know, each time I was telling the story, even in church on Sunday morning, the man with the white guitar was dead. He had been murdered soon after we had talked, killed by someone in his own community.

The first I knew of this was when I saw his face appear on a television news report several nights later. At that moment I was so overwhelmed. I had stood with this 37-year-old man during our cross vigil and had shared with him the meaning of John 3:16, yet not long afterwards he had been murdered. I'm glad, that if only for the man with the white guitar, we stood at that spot with the cross. I'm glad he saw the cross with JOHN 3:16, I'm glad he shouted to us, I'm glad he asked what John 3:16 was, and I'm glad he allowed me to explain it to him. Soon after this I spoke with his family who told me they had taken great comfort in knowing I was with him before he was murdered and that he listened to me as I explained the Bible to him.

The Cross of Crosses

At the end of the 2011 CU@ theCROSS event, we had left the 20ft cross in place between the gates. As explained above, it remained there for three years, but then succumbed to the weather and fell. This time, at the end of 39+1 we decided to leave another cross between the dividing gates, but only this time it would be one that would last - the *Cross of Crosses* would be made from Corten Steel. The reason for the name is that this is one large cross with 45 smaller crosses cut out of it. The 45 smaller crosses represent the years of conflict in Northern Ireland from 1969 until 2014, and illustrates the fact that people were killed during each of those 45 years. Over 3,700 lost their lives - the one large cross of iron represents the fact that one died for all regardless of religious, cultural or ethnic background.

The *Cross of Crosses* was unveiled on Good Friday after the *cross walks* and after the cross vigils had all ended. We'd chosen a 16-year-old boy from the Catholic community and a 16-year-old girl from the Protestant community to jointly unveil the cross, because Good Friday 2014 was the 16th anniversary of our peace agreement, yet people were still being murdered on our streets. The appeal to the community, by the unveiling of the *Cross of Crosses*, and to those who would still use violence to achieve their aims, was to let 2014 be the year when violence would end for good. The media, even the so-called biggest radio show in Northern Ireland, showed no interest in this event or its symbolism and significance.

Sadly however, a man who had sat in a hut within the Catholic community and who saw the cross being carried past him every day for 40 days, was shot dead in that same hut about 90 minutes after the *Cross of Crosses* had been unveiled that Good Friday afternoon.

The media swarmed to show interest in this tragic murder, as it did again a week later when a young teenage student was stabbed to death by another student just yards from where the *Cross of Crosses* stands.

The *Cross of Crosses* was designed by Northern Ireland artist Ross Wilson who provided his services free of charge; it was made and supplied at net price by Smyth Engineering Ltd in Garvagh and was personally delivered and installed by James Smyth the owner of the company; the cost of supply was provided by George McIlroy on behalf of IGNITE, an outreach in 2013 at the Waterfront Hall to the hurting and the broken.

And so 39+1 came to an end when once again the cross was raised throughout the city and beyond, witnessed hundreds of thousands of times by pedestrians and by motorists. We prayed, we worshipped, we witnessed, we laughed, and we wept; lives were changed and lives were lost, but we were out there.

The cross still stands

Some six months after 39+1, a grenade attack was launched at police officers who stood on the very spot where we had stood with the cross for those 40 days, the same place where the man with the white guitar had called out to us. At that time I received a message from Ronnie O'Neill who had stood with us at that very spot during 39+1. He suggested we go back to the same place and stand with the cross for a few days. We agreed to do so, but this time we noticed a huge concrete block with a tin bucket fixed in its centre. So on the last day, four days later, I stood holding the cross in the bucket, and with police security cameras focused down on us, and as I held the cross in place, Ronnie poured quick-drying concrete into the bucket so that within 15 minutes the cross was firmly embedded in concrete.

Within one year, the cross with JOHN 3:16 emblazoned on it has been seen by many thousands of passers-by. There it stands in one of the most volatile areas of Belfast, standing between two conflicting communities, being a silent witness to the violence that has surrounded it at times, but not knowing if it might be purposely uprooted by those opposed to its message, or if it might succumb to the upsurge of violence that raises its ugly head at various times throughout the year.

During one of those waves of violence, in July 2015, the security forces erected a temporary steel barrier alongside the cross for the purpose of keeping opposing factions apart. There it stood on the dividing line, stretching out to both sides of the community amid the ongoing conflict and silently appealing for reconciliation and peace. Both sides showed great respect for the cross, but they equally rejected its appeal. Violence broke out close to and around the cross with several people injured while others were arrested near the cross.

I was in the USA at that particular time, but was staying in touch with the unfolding developments. While hearing and reading about the unrest in Belfast, I received a photograph with the accompanying message, 'The Cross Still Stands.' That's the message that continues to emanate from Northern Ireland, that regardless of the historical conflict, and regardless of sectarian unrest - the cross still stands. Why? Because there are enough people who have what it takes to ensure that the cross stands firm and that its message is never silenced.

Chapter 28

Have You Got What it Takes?

New Life City Church is not where it is as a church, because everything was handed to us on a platter, but we are where we are as a church in spite of the fact that nothing was ever simply handed to us. As stated previously, we are not where we are, because someone stepped up and handed us a cheque for a million pounds, but we are where we are in spite of the fact that no one ever did hand us that cheque. No, we are where we are today, because of leaders and because of people who have what it takes.

Becoming a Christian is a simple step, but being a Christian is the challenge. I thank God for those around us who have responded to that challenge. Some from relatively simple backgrounds, while others are from more complicated backgrounds, yet all are equally important. In the midst of writing this book, one night while sitting casually with others in our coffee shop, I noticed that sitting chatting and drinking coffee together were five men, one of whom was a former member of the UDR; one a former member of the RUC (Royal Ulster Constabulary – Police); one a former member of the UFF (Ulster Freedom Fighters); and one whose uncle was at one time a senior and very active member of the IRA. Yet there we all sat, former enemies, but reconciled in Christ.

On my most recent return from the USA I called at the church on my first day home. You would expect to be welcomed by someone saying: "Hi ya Pastor, welcome home," but no, not this pastor! The very first words spoken to me as I walked towards the door were: "Here comes the UDR man!" These were spoken tongue in cheek by the former IRA man mentioned above. We laughed at that moment, but as I walked on into the coffee shop I thought to myself, man, these are changed days! Thank God for the change He has made.

You see church starts with an individual. That individual is not someone else, it's you and it's me. So, no matter where you live or what you face, be it sectarianism, racism, opposition or persecution, the question needs to be asked, 'Do you have what it takes?'

For some, the primary question needing answering is, are you born-again? Not do you attend church? But do you know Jesus in a personal way? Do you know him as your Lord and Saviour? If the answer is no or that you're not sure, but you would like to know for certain, let me pray this prayer with you:

Dear Lord Jesus, thank you for loving me.

Thank you for dying in my place and for my sins.

I ask you to forgive me and to cleanse me of all my sins.

Come into my life and be my Lord and my Saviour,

and help me to follow you from this day forward. Amen.

Once you have prayed that prayer the Holy Spirit comes to live within you. John wrote, *'The one who is in you is greater than the one who is in the world'* (1 John 4:4), and Paul wrote, *'If God is for us, who can be against us?'* (Romans 8:31). So yes, once you are born-again you actually do have what it takes, because of the Spirit of God who now lives within you.

Moses tried in his own strength to deliver his people from

Egypt (Exodus 2:12) but it was only after God became real to him (Exodus 3:2) did he then have what it takes. He went from knowing about God to yielding to Him. Gideon hid in a winepress (Judges 6:11) from the Midianites, but when he experienced God he could not hide any further. God used him to deliver his people! David had been anointed King by the prophet Samuel (Samuel 16:13), and although he made mistakes, God said he was, *'a man after my own heart!'* (Samuel 13:14) Why? Because even though he failed, he continually turned to God, which is what we must do.

Every person in the Bible at one point did not have what it takes. But when we yield to the Holy Spirit we become those who have what it takes, like Daniel, Ruth, John the Baptist, Mary, Stephen, Paul, all those in the upper room, and the promise still stands…

"For the promise is for you and for your children and for all who are far off, for all whom the Lord our God will call." Acts 2:39

If God is with you, then you have what it takes.

Final comments – raising and releasing others

As Pastor of New Life City Church I thank God for opening my eyes to enable me to see ministry is not about me but about God. It is not how many times I stand on a platform, but can I stand on God's platform in the midst of a hostile world, facing criticism and opposition, and still uphold the message of the cross no matter the price. Hollywood may have entered the church with all its glam and glitter, but when the day is over, when the curtains are closed, and when no one is looking – do you still have what it takes?

Godly leaders are not in it for the 'title', but are like anyone else who follows God – they are followers and disciples – nothing more, nothing less. Like all followers and disciples of Jesus Christ they are advancing the objectives of the Kingdom of God, because they've got what it takes – they have learned to yield to the Spirit of God. I thank God for worship leaders, singers and musicians that can help us get beyond the outer court, prayer warriors, intercessors and evangelists who touch heaven and who touch people's lives. I thank God for ministry teams and for help teams who often go beyond the call of duty, with each one having what it takes to touch their neighbour, village, city and beyond.

Thank God for Christian leaders who are focused on getting believers to where they need to be within church and within life in general; who are helping advance the Kingdom of God in the face of hostility, and who continue to lift the message of the cross whatever the circumstances, and who do so because they have what it takes, which is Christ in them, their hope and strength.

There are many leaders who are where they are and do what they do, because they have what it takes to lead from the front; to lead by example; to influence, inspire and motivate. They fully recognise they are not called to attract people to themselves, but to attract them to Christ; they are not called to simply draw people into church services and to settle down as attenders, but to enable them to be the church and prepare them to go as the church; they are not called to fill buildings with members, but to fill the world with disciples. God is still asking the question: *"Who shall I send, who will go for us?"* I for one continue to say: Lord here am I, send me," but I've never gone alone.

We started this book with the question, and as we end I pray you will yield yourself to God, and that you will realise it never was about you or me, but it was and it is only about God.

Can I ask: 'Have you got what it takes?'

If God is in us then the answer is 'YES!' For Scripture says... *"Not by might nor by power, but by my Spirit," says the LORD Almighty* (Zechariah 4:6).

Time to step up and do what it takes!

To contact Pastor Jack or invite him to minister in your area, contact him using the following details:

New Life City Church
143 Northumberland Street
BELFAST
Northern Ireland
BT13 2JF

Telephone
Inside UK: 028 9023 9572
Outside UK: 0044 28 9023 9572

www.NewLifeBelfast.org
pastorjack.newlife@gmail.com
Facebook: New-Life-City-Church-63413876395
Twitter: NLCCmedia

Ever thought of publishing a book?

Contact

Maurice Wylie Media

www.MauriceWylieMedia.com

sales@mauricewyliemedia.com

CPSIA information can be obtained at www.ICGtesting.com
Printed in the USA
BVOW06s1809290916

463587BV00003B/7/P